Paraprofessionals and Teachers Working Together

Highly Effective Strategies for Inclusive Classrooms

Second Edition

Susan Gingras Fitzell, M.Ed.

Library of Congress Cataloging-in-Publication Data

Fitzell, Susan Gingras
   Paraprofessionals and Teachers Working Together -- 2nd ed. 153 pp.
ISBN 978-1-932995-07-7

At the time of publication, the information cited within is the most current available and/or the original source material. The author and publisher do not provide any guarantee or warranty regarding the information provided by any sources cited here, nor do we take responsibility for any changes to information or Web sites. If you find an error or would like to alert us to a change to any resource cited herein, please contact us online: http://aimhieducational.com/ContactUs.asp. We encourage parents and teachers to closely monitor Internet usage by children and students.

If you have questions or would like customized school in-service or ongoing consultation, contact:
Susan Gingras Fitzell
PO Box 6182
Manchester, NH 03108-6182
Phone: 603-625-6087 or 210-473-2863
Email: SFitzell@SusanFitzell.com
Main Website: http://www.SusanFitzell.com
Interactive Blog & Teacher Resource: http://www.HighTestScores.org
Facebook: http://www.facebook.com/SusanFitzellfb
YouTube: http://www.youtube.com/susanfitzell
Twitter: http://twitter.com/susanfitzell

For supplemental handouts and information:
http://www.aimhieducational.com/inclusion.aspx

DEDICATION

To Norma Sanchez, Kathy Wicker, Ginger Davis, Bethany Moody, Yvette Kazynski, and Mary Ellen McGrath; outstanding paraprofessionals who I was blessed to work with over the years.

TABLE OF CONTENTS

PART 1: THE ORGANIZATION OF COLLABORATION 1

COMMUNICATION AND AN ORGANIZED APPROACH 2

DEFINING THE ROLE OF THE PARAPROFESSIONAL 4

LEAST EFFECTIVE USE OF PARAEDUCATOR'S SKILLS 4

WAYS PARAPROFESSIONALS SUPPORT INCLUSIVE CLASSROOMS 4

One to One Assistant – Page 1 5

Small Group Assistance 7

Social/Behavioral Assistance 8

Academic Assistance – Page 1 9

Physical Assistance 11

Teacher Support 12

TIPS FOR SUCCESS- PARAEDUCATOR 13

TIPS FOR SUCCESS- TEACHER: GENERAL AND SPECIAL ED 14

CUEING STRATEGIES 16

THE PARAPROFESSIONAL: A COLLECTOR OF INFORMATION 17

Ways to Collect Data 17

Data Collection Considerations 17

Data Collection Form 1 - Elementary 19

Data Collection Form 2 - Secondary 20

DIFFERENTIATING ROLES-A LEGAL PRIORITY 21

CONCERNS ON WHICH TO REACH AGREEMENT 22

Lesson Planning 22

Instruction 22

Student Behavior 23

Communication 23

THE DAILY SCHEDULE 24

SCHEDULING IN THE ELEMENTARY SCHOOL 24

SCHEDULING AT THE SECONDARY LEVEL 24

Sample Secondary Level Daily Schedule – Multiple Locations 26

Elementary Level Daily Schedule –Single Location 29

HOW DO I FOLLOW-UP OUTSIDE OF CLASS? 30

SAMPLE LETTERS TO ASSIST WITH FOLLOW-UP 30

Secondary Level 30

KEEPING UP WITH THE IEP 33

Class List Adaptations Chart 33
IEP-Based Planning Forms 35

PART 2: COLLABORATION 36

POTENTIAL ROADBLOCKS: DIFFERENCES 37

TEACHING (AND RE-TEACHING) METHODOLOGY 37
PERSONALITY DIFFERENCES 37
COMFORT ZONES 38
LEGAL WORRIES 38
THIS IS NOT THE WAY IT SHOULD BE 39
FEELINGS OF INTIMIDATION 39
CREDIBILITY 40
INSUFFICIENT TIME 40
LACK OF ADMINISTRATIVE SUPPORT 41
POTENTIAL ROADBLOCKS: OTHER PRACTICALITIES 41

OVERCOMING ROADBLOCKS: SOLUTIONS 42

BE FLEXIBLE 42
IDENTIFY AND FOCUS ON YOUR PARAPROFESSIONAL'S STRENGTHS 42
ADOPT A "THEY ARE ALL OUR STUDENTS" ATTITUDE 42
OVERCOMING ROADBLOCKS: SUMMARY & MORE 43

PERCEPTIONS & PERSONALITY 44

LOOKING AT PERSONALITY TYPES 44

PERSONALITY PREFERENCE AND LEARNING STYLE 47

Characteristics of Personality Type (Myers-Briggs) 47
Extraversion (E) versus Introversion (I) 47
Sensing (S) versus Intuition (N) 48
Thinking (T) versus Feeling (F) 48
Judging (J) versus Perceptive (P) 48
MBTI Self Assessment Table 49
The MBTI Type Table 50

WHEN IN CONFLICT 52

STOPPING CONFLICT IN ITS TRACKS! 54

STOPPING CONFLICT IN ITS TRACKS 55

Comebacks that don't escalate the conflict 55

COMMUNICATION: "WHAT'S WORKING?" CARD..56
   Tips for Successful Collaboration..*56*
   Pick-Me-Ups, Pick-U-Ups..*56*

PART 3: POSITIVE BEHAVIOR MANAGEMENT **57**

BE A POSITIVE ROLE MODEL..**58**
  BELIEFS AND ATTITUDES OF THE ROLE MODEL 58
  THE ROLE MODEL AND DISCIPLINE 58
  TREAT YOUTH WITH RESPECT 59

SPECIAL CONSIDERATIONS FOR THE PARAPROFESSIONAL.................**62**
  WORKING WITHIN THE PARAPROFESSIONAL'S JURISDICTION 62
  VIOLENT STUDENTS: PROCEED WITH CAUTION 62
  GENERAL BEHAVIOR MANAGEMENT TIPS 63
   Behaviors to Avoid When Disciplining....................................*63*
   Techniques That Build Rapport & Foster Better Behavior................*63*

CHOICE: ENCOURAGE CHOICE AND DECISION-MAKING....................**64**
  SCRIPTS FOR OFFERING CHOICE...64
  POSSIBLE SCRIPTS FOR RESPONDING TO STUDENT BEHAVIOR 66

BEHAVIORAL SUPPORT STRATEGIES FOR THE PLAYGROUND AND CAFETERIA **68**
   Playground Strategies...*69*

BEHAVIOR MANAGEMENT FOR 1-1 & SMALL GROUPS......................**70**
  CUEING STUDENTS TO REDIRECT OR REINFORCE 70
   Behavior Management Cue Card...*71*
  STRATEGIC IGNORING...72
  PROXIMITY CONTROL..72
  COMMUNICATION COULD BE THE SOLUTION! 72

TIPS & TOOLS TO FOCUS AND CALM STUDENTS **75**
   For Students Having Difficulty with Attention and Distractibility..........*75*
   Brain Gym®: A Wakeup Call to the Brain.................................*76*
   "Hook-Ups"...*77*
   Mandalas: Focus, Calm, and Creative Inspiration........................*78*
   Color Your Own Mandala..*79*
  DEALING WITH TATTLING..80
   The Difference between Tattling and Telling...............................*81*

PART 4: ACADEMIC SUPPORT 82

UNDERSTANDING SPECIAL NEEDS 83

WHAT IS EXCEPTIONALITY UNDER FEDERAL LAW? 83
 Assessment and Federal Law *83*
WHAT IS A SPECIFIC LEARNING DISABILITY? 84
FUNCTIONAL LIMITATIONS 85
RELATED TERMINOLOGY 86

HOW THE BRAIN LEARNS 89

MULTIPLE INTELLIGENCE / LEARNING STYLE 90

ASSESSMENT CHECKLIST FOR MULTIPLE INTELLIGENCE 90
 Suggestions for Learning according to Multiple Intelligence *93*

SETTING UP THE ENVIRONMENT 94

STRATEGIES TO ASSIST WITH MEMORIZATION 95

PAPER AND PENCIL STRATEGIES 95
MIND & BODY CONNECTION STRATEGIES 96
TEACHING EACH OTHER 97
MUSIC AS A STRATEGY 98
MIND MAPPING/GRAPHIC ROADMAPS/VISUAL ORGANIZERS 99
MNEMONIC DEVICES 101
 Associations *101*
 Rhyming *102*
 Chunking *102*
 Acronyms *103*
 Acrostics *103*
SEQUENCING STRATEGY 106
DRAWING, COLOR, AND MEMORY 106
 The Meaning of Color *107*
 Draw It So You'll Know It *107*
DRILL AND PRACTICE STRATEGIES 108
 The Fitzpell Method of Studying Spelling Words *108*
 Three Card Match: Review *110*
MAKE IT MEANINGFUL 112

STRATEGIES TO ASSIST WITH WRITING ASSIGNMENTS 113

WRITING STRATEGIES 113
CLUSTERING ACTIVITY STEP ONE 114
 Method for Writing Better Sentences *122*

STRATEGIES TO ASSIST WITH READING ASSIGNMENTS..........................123

HIGHLIGHTING ACTIVITY 123
POST-IT® NOTE METHOD OF "HIGHLIGHTING" 124

MATH TIP FOR SPATIAL DIFFICULTIES 125

MAKING ASSIGNMENTS EASIER TO ACCOMPLISH 126

CURRENT EVENTS...127
BOOK REPORT 128

STUDY TOOLS AND ORGANIZERS 132

NOTE-TAKING STRATEGIES 132
Cut and Paste Notes Using Mind Maps and Charts...........................*132*
THREE-COLUMN NOTE PAPER 134
GRADE REVIEW SHEET...135
ADD CHECKBOXES: 136
USE MSWORD READABILITY STATISTICS TO IMPROVE WRITING 137
AUTOSUMMARIZE IN MSWORD 139

DIFFICULTY/ADAPTATION QUICK LIST 140

WORLD WIDE WEB RESOURCES 141

ORDER SUSAN'S BOOKS! 142

NOTES 144

Part 1: The Organization of Collaboration

Communication and an Organized Approach

One of the most important aspects of an effective working relationship between the paraprofessional, special educator, teacher, or specialist is clear and consistent communication and organization. It is critical to communicate frequently and use organizing tools that can help define roles, define expectations, and set parameters for class norms as part of the communication process. Why is structure and time to talk so important? Because without having a system in place to discuss issues, organize information, and handle variables, much is subject to guesswork, and guesswork often causes problems and communication breakdown.

A paraprofessional[1] often enters the classroom with a tremendous amount of concern about intruding on the teacher's space. Many times this concern can lead to inaction, a lesser quality of experience for both the paraeducator and teacher, and sometimes can even lead to feelings of intimidation. Time spent communicating—establishing rapport, documenting and organizing roles, expectations, and schedules—can make the difference between a harmonious relationship and one filled with discord.

It is important for both teachers and paraeducators to understand that a paraprofessional's job is demanding and varies tremendously from one class to the other. He may not know what he will encounter in any one situation, what he will be required to do once he walks in that classroom door, or what personalities he may have to navigate.

One of the trickiest parts of working in the classroom as a paraprofessional is understanding the paraprofessional's role. What is that role? The paraprofessional's role is determined by each student's needs, whether they are academic needs or behavioral needs, and often these are dictated by the Individual Education Plan (IEP) or the special education department. Sometimes a paraprofessional is working with one single student. Other times, a paraprofessional may be working with an entire class of students. In that situation, the paraprofessional may be working as a classroom assistant because many students in the classroom are on an IEP.

---

[1] Paraprofessional, paraeducator, teacher assistant, teacher aide, etc. are used interchangeably in education. This text will use paraprofessional and paraeducator to refer to this job title.

It is very difficult in these situations to walk into a classroom without any prior dialogue as to what the paraprofessional's roles and responsibilities will include. The paraprofessional's job is to support and assist students within the classroom using the IEPs of the student, or several students, involved to provide the framework. The supervising special or general education teacher is responsible for direct instruction, providing assistance, and guiding the paraprofessional to work effectively with individual students.

Being a paraeducator is a rewarding job because paraprofessionals make a positive difference in children's, youths', and teenagers' lives. It is important that the paraprofessional feels positive about the work he or she is doing and feels in harmony with the classroom teacher.

Defining the Role of the Paraprofessional

Least Effective Use of Paraeducator's Skills

The general education teacher and students both lose a valuable resource if the paraprofessional's role is to:
- Photocopy papers

- Copy notes (solely)

- Run errands

- Hold up the back wall of the classroom, figuratively speaking.

Ways Paraprofessionals Support Inclusive Classrooms

The ways a paraprofessional might assist in the classroom are as individual as the students they are responsible for, the classrooms they work in, and the grade level they teach. On the following pages are checklists filled with options for the general education teacher, the special education teacher, and the paraprofessional to consider when defining paraprofessional roles in the classroom.

Use these checklists as a tool to negotiate the working relationship in the classroom before the paraprofessional starts "on the job."

One to One Assistant – Page 1

Classroom Teacher: _____

Subject: _____

Student Initials:_____

- ☐ Sometimes work with individual students one-on-one.

- ☐ Support student in getting ready for in-class assignments or for other activities so he or she can keep up with the class while at the same time learning how to become more independent.

- ☐ Substitute activities without changing curriculum.

- ☐ Adapt instructional materials in accordance with the IEP.

- ☐ Re-teach instruction and provide reinforcement.

- ☐ Assist the student with individual activities.

- ☐ Help student with makeup work.

- ☐ Assist student with interpreting and following directions.

- ☐ Modify assignments as directed by the special education teacher or the general education teacher.

- ☐ Make on-the-spot adaptations to curriculum and instruction according to pre-established guidelines.

- ☐ Administer tests individually reinforcing skills that the teacher previously taught.

- ☐ Read aloud to the students.

- ☐ Assist with organizational skills.

One to One Assistant – Page 2

- ☐ Create educational memory games and activities.

- ☐ Keep records to document behavior of individual students.

- ☐ Maintain a daily journal or log communicating with parents or other classroom teachers regarding class work, homework, or daily activities.

- ☐ Facilitate social opportunities and interactions for all students.

- ☐ Supervise student who might leave the classroom for a break or might leave to go to another classroom.

- ☐ Check for work completion and homework.

- ☐ Copy notes occasionally or assist with note taking.

- ☐ Support student when involved with group work.

- ☐ Cue/refocus/redirect student.

- ☐ Photocopy overheads and/or make photocopies of notes.

- ☐ Create review worksheets.

- ☐ Assist with the testing process.

- ☐ Read aloud to the student.

- ☐ Use Boardmaker® (Mayer-Johnson) or find clipart pictures to assist student's ability to communicate. Create a "find and point" communication tool for the student.

- ☐ Help create "social stories" for student (autistic spectrum).

- ☐ Create a picture schedule list, color-coded, and teach the student to be as independent as possible with this schedule.

- ☐ Enlist peers to help the student gather and carry materials.

- ☐ _____

- ☐ _____

Small Group Assistance

Classroom Teacher: _____

Subject: _____

Student Initials: _____

- ☐ Substitute activities without changing curriculum.
- ☐ Adapt instructional materials in accordance with the IEP.
- ☐ Provide remedial instruction and reinforcement skills.
- ☐ Assist the students with individual activities.
- ☐ Help students with makeup work.
- ☐ Assist students with interpreting and following directions.
- ☐ Make on-the-spot adaptations to curriculum and instruction according to pre-established guidelines.
- ☐ Assist with organizational skills.
- ☐ Check for work completion or homework.
- ☐ Create educational memory games and activities.
- ☐ Conduct learning activities as directed by the classroom teacher.
- ☐ Facilitate social opportunities and interactions.
- ☐ Support students involved with group work.
- ☐ Cue, refocus, or redirect students.
- ☐ Read aloud to students.
- ☐ Review for tests.

- ☐ _____

- ☐ _____

- ☐ _____

- ☐ _____

- ☐ _____

- ☐ _____

- ☐ _____

- ☐ _____

Social/Behavioral Assistance

Classroom Teacher: _____

Subject: _____

Student Initials: _____

Behavioral Assistance
- ☐ Cue, refocus, or redirect students.
- ☐ Implement position control (positioning oneself in the classroom as a behavior management strategy).
- ☐ Help create "social stories" for students in the autistic spectrum.
- ☐ Assist with classroom management by implementing class rules.
- ☐ Keep records to document behavior of individual students.
- ☐ Supervise students who might leave the classroom for break or might leave to go to another classroom.
- ☐ Supervise individual students or groups of students at various times of day, such as lunch, recess, or when the teacher is out of the room.
- ☐ Supervise students during lunch, recess, assemblies, or when getting on or off the bus.

- ☐ _____
- ☐ _____
- ☐ _____

Social Assistance
- ☐ Create a picture schedule list, color-coded, and teach the student to be as independent as possible with this schedule.
- ☐ Enlist peers to help a student gather and carry materials.
- ☐ Facilitate social opportunities and interactions for all students.

- ☐ _____
- ☐ _____
- ☐ _____
- ☐ _____

Academic Assistance – Page 1

Classroom Teacher: _____

Subject: _____

Student Initials: _____

- ☐ Support student in getting ready for in-class assignments or other activities so he or she can keep up with the class while, at the same time, learning how to become more independent.
- ☐ Monitor the student's level of participation in the classroom.
- ☐ Substitute activities without changing curriculum.
- ☐ Help the classroom teacher with instructional strategies or other supports that are required in the IEP.
- ☐ Adapt instructional materials in accordance with the IEP.
- ☐ Provide remedial instruction and reinforcement skills.
- ☐ Assist students with individual activities.
- ☐ Help students with makeup work.
- ☐ Assist students with interpreting and following directions.
- ☐ Modify assignments for specific students as directed by the special education teacher or the general education teacher.
- ☐ Make on-the-spot adaptations to curriculum and instruction according to pre-established guidelines.
- ☐ Administer tests individually.
- ☐ Reinforce skills that the teacher previously taught.
- ☐ Read aloud to the students.
- ☐ Assist with organizational skills.
- ☐ Check for work completion or homework.
- ☐ Create educational memory games and activities.
- ☐ Conduct learning activities as directed by the classroom teacher for a small group of students.
- ☐ Maintain a daily journal or log communicating with parents or other classroom teachers regarding class work, homework, or daily activities.
- ☐ Copy notes occasionally or assist with note taking.
- ☐ Support students involved with group work.
- ☐ _____
- ☐ _____

Academic Assistance – Page 2

- ☐ Photocopy overheads and/or make copies of notes.
- ☐ Create review worksheets.
- ☐ Assist with the testing process.
- ☐ Follow up with the student outside the classroom.
- ☐ Motivate and support students with homework.
- ☐ Work with drop-in center, learning center, or resource room to help students focus and stay on track.
- ☐ Ask questions in class.
- ☐ Answer questions in class.
- ☐ Read orally (low-level readers).
- ☐ Review for tests with small groups of students.
- ☐ Guide student-centered activities.
- ☐ Use Boardmaker® (Mayer-Johnson) or find clipart pictures to assist student's ability to communicate. Create a "find and point" communication tool for the student.
- ☐ Serve as a scribe.

- ☐ _____
- ☐ _____
- ☐ _____
- ☐ _____
- ☐ _____
- ☐ _____
- ☐ _____
- ☐ _____
- ☐ _____
- ☐ _____
- ☐ _____

Physical Assistance

Classroom Teacher: _____

Subject: _____

Student Initials: _____

- ☐ Serve as a personal care attendant when appropriate.
- ☐ Assist with personal hygiene, including feeding and diapering.
- ☐ Assist students with motor or mobility limitations.
- ☐ Assist students with individual activities.
- ☐ Maintain a daily journal or log communicating with parents or other classroom teachers regarding class work, homework, or daily activities.
- ☐ Supervise students who might leave the classroom for break or might leave to go to another classroom.
- ☐ Supervise individual students or groups of students at various times of day, such as at lunch, recess, or when the teacher is out of the room.
- ☐ Supervise students during lunch, recess, assemblies, or when getting on or off the bus.
- ☐ Use Boardmaker® (Mayer-Johnson) or find clipart pictures to assist student's ability to communicate. Create a "find and point" communication tool for the student.
- ☐ Serve as a scribe.

- ☐ _____
- ☐ _____
- ☐ _____
- ☐ _____
- ☐ _____
- ☐ _____
- ☐ _____
- ☐ _____
- ☐ _____

Teacher Support

Classroom Teacher: _____

Subject: _____

Student Initials: _____

☐ Help the classroom teacher with instructional strategies or other supports that are required in the IEP.

☐ Conduct learning activities as directed by the classroom teacher for a small group of students.

☐ Make instructional materials for the whole class so that the teacher can work with individual students.

☐ Supervise individual students or groups of students at various times of day, such as at lunch, recess, or when the teacher is out of the room.

☐ Supervise students during lunch, recess, assemblies, or when getting on or off the bus.

☐ Photocopy overheads and/or make copies of notes.

☐ Create review worksheets.

☐ Assist with the testing process.

☐ Answer questions in class.

☐ Implement position control (positioning oneself in the classroom as a behavior management strategy).

☐ Guide student-centered activities.

☐ Assist with classroom management by implementing classroom rules.

☐ _____

☐ _____

☐ _____

☐ _____

☐ _____

☐ _____

☐ _____

Tips for Success- Paraeducator

- Encourage students to make friendships in the classroom so they feel empowered and learn to be more independent.
- Position yourself so that the teacher communicates directly with the student, enabling them to develop a rapport.
- Encourage other students to interact with students with special needs.
- Ensure that students own their behavior by using strategies and language that takes the responsibility off you and keeps it where it belongs – on the child.
- Ask questions. It is helpful to the teacher and to other students in class. Feel free to offer suggestions. At times, you may want to offer them to the teacher privately; however, offering suggestions appropriately in the classroom is a wonderful advantage to the class as a whole.
- Get help when you need it. Everyone needs help at times.
- Allow and encourage students to do anything and everything they can and should do for themselves. If we fall into the trap of doing too much for the child, we encourage learned helplessness.
- Be flexible.
- Consider yourself a helper to all students in the classroom. This benefits the teacher, reduces stigma on the student with specials needs, and supports all students in the room.
- Move around the room. At times, it will be necessary and critical to be near your assigned student(s). However, it is just as critical for student(s) to be on their own in order to develop independence.
- Try to remember that no matter what the cognitive age of the child, it is important to treat him or her socially in accordance with his or her chronological age. The more we expect, the more they will deliver, within reason.
- Expect and encourage age-appropriate social behavior.
- Feel comfortable explaining any child's disability to other children in terms they will understand as appropriate in the classroom. Consult confidentiality laws to determine appropriateness.
- Identify and rally your strengths. You have expertise that benefits the child and the teacher in the classroom. Use it.
- Ask yourself, "How would I feel if I had an adult right next to me all day long?" Have the courage to give students personal space to interact with the classroom teacher, other students, and to work independently.

- When you must make quick, on-the-spot decisions or adaptations while providing instructions, it is critical to discuss these decisions with the general and/or special education teacher as soon as possible so they can provide necessary feedback.

Tips for Success- Teacher: General and Special Ed

- Consider the paraprofessional an essential member of your teaching team. Whenever possible, include the paraprofessional in planning, team meetings, troubleshooting, and any other decision where you feel input from the paraprofessional may be valuable. Paraprofessionals in my world are just as human as I am. I always treated my paraprofessionals with respect and as equals, and that always enhanced my relationships and the effectiveness of the paraprofessionals in my classroom.
- Empower the paraprofessional to monitor behavior and support the discipline process in the classroom. This empowerment will be worth millions when you must leave the classroom with a substitute, knowing that you have challenging students in the room. You will be able to rest more comfortably knowing that the paraprofessional can handle the class and that students will respect that person's authority.
- Teach the paraprofessional how to handle discipline issues in your classroom.
- Discuss your goals, your priorities, and plans with your paraprofessionals on a daily basis. Sometimes this may mean stealing a few minutes of time before class, while students are doing a quiet seat activity, or after class. Communication is critical, not only to the success of students in the classroom, but also to the teaching relationship.
- Provide the paraprofessional with lesson plans, activities, or "to do" items as soon as possible. Last minute rushes often stress the paraprofessional and do not allow for proper preparation time.
- Discuss issues with your paraprofessional, especially when the issue is related to the student he or she is working with. Oftentimes a paraprofessional has an outside view that we as teachers tend to miss. Their ideas and possible solutions could be invaluable in a difficult situation.
- Inform the paraprofessional of critical information regarding students he or she is involved with or information that could affect classroom dynamics. Ask the paraprofessional what he or she needs to know in order to do the job most effectively.

- Avoid interruption when the paraeducator is working with a student or several students. Interruption undermines the paraprofessional's authority with the students, and often causes distress and possible conflict.
- Have a welcome interview with your team. For example, a team might include a special educator, the general educator, and a paraprofessional. Learn more about one another and develop an initial understanding of your roles and responsibilities.
- Take notes and document those notes on easy-to-remember or easy-to-use forms so that they can be referred to throughout the year. This is critical for paraprofessionals who are working with more than one teacher, because each teacher may have different expectations.
- Compile a loose-leaf binder for the paraprofessional that contains class rules, expectations, a syllabus, etc.
- Model how you want things done. For example, model for the paraprofessional how to administer tests.
- Model the difference between "cueing" a student to remember an answer vs. giving the student the answer.
- Model/teach how to respond to specific behavior.
- Provide scripts when necessary to assist the paraprofessional in responding to student behavior.

Cueing Strategies

1. <u>CUE</u>: Point out what is 'right' in student's response. Then take the student back to the 'instructional moment' so they can visualize the lesson. The visualization may cue the student's memory.

2. <u>PROMPT</u>: Give a verbal prompt to trigger student's memory for connections or associations that will facilitate recall. For example:

   - Question: "What is the symbol for Mercury?"
   - Student: "I don't know."
   - Prompt: "Hug (Hg) a thermometer and it'll get hot!"

3. <u>CLUE</u>: Give a verbal or nonverbal hint such as a key word, beginning sound, etc. to prod student's memory.

   - Question: "What is the symbol for Mercury?"
   - Student: "Mc?"
   - Prompt: "No; it starts with an 'H'."

4. <u>CLARIFY</u>: Ask a probing question to encourage students to elaborate and enhance their answer with more details and less imprecision.

   - Question: "Should society have the right to tell you how to behave on your own time?"
   - Student: "No. It causes other problems."
   - Prompt: "What kind of problems? Can you give examples?"

5. <u>PROBE</u>: Ask question(s) that guide a student toward making a more complete or appropriate response.

   - Question: "What is the cause of our ozone depletion?"
   - Student: "Chlorofluorocarbons."
   - Prompt: "How do you know chlorofluorocarbons are destroying the ozone layer?"

The Paraprofessional: A Collector of Information

Paraprofessionals often have one-on-one contact with students that gives them insights into what is happening with the students on a daily basis that most other people in a student's life would not necessarily notice. The paraprofessional may observe behaviors, may be privy to attitudes, and may understand motivations or obstacles the student faces better than any other professional in the building. Sometimes, the paraprofessional can even help parents (when appropriate) gain some needed insight on how the student is doing and what the student is showing in terms of behavior.

The paraprofessional who documents this "data" provides a valuable service for the IEP process. Sometimes a paraprofessional, as part of his or her job, is actually required to keep track of student progress, log behavior, and report that behavior to other appropriate staff members.

Ways to Collect Data

- Have students self assess.
- Keep a notebook or journal to track objective thoughts and observations. Stick to the facts. Opinions are best left unwritten.
- Customize a form that suits each individual situation or student in order to track information easily.
- Keep a portfolio of student work or samples to display how the student is progressing.

Data Collection Considerations

Consider the following core questions in regards to what data to collect.

- What is the goal of collecting this information? For example, is the goal to document behavior? To monitor progress toward IEP goals and objectives? To determine which adaptations or modifications work best? Or to determine what may or may not be working?
- What types of information do I need to collect to reach the goal? What is the function of the student's behavior? What do you think the student is getting out of his or her behavior? What is the "antecedent" to the student's

behavior? (Information about the student's activities, social skills, physical needs, and emotional well-being, etc. is good to include.)

- Am I responsible for summarizing the data and writing the report?
- When should I be gathering this information? How often? Under what conditions?
- How will this information be used? Where will this information be used, and under what circumstances will it be used? Will it be used in an IEP meeting? Will it be for the parents' benefit? Will it be used by the classroom teacher? The special educator? The administrator?
- Who may see this information? (Consult with the Special Education supervisor to find out who will be able to access this information.)
- Make sure that the information collected adheres to confidentiality laws, respects the student's and parents' sensitivities, and does not hurt or hinder the education or progress of the student.
- If data being collected makes you uncomfortable, it is important to address this issue with your supervisor. Do not do anything you are uncomfortable with without analyzing the reasons for your discomfort and making an informed decision on how to move forward. Listen to the red flags that go up in your mind and in your heart.
- For your safety and the legal safety of the school, stick to the FACTS. Avoid writing down your opinions, feelings, conclusions, theories, etc. Save those things for when the time is appropriate to discuss them. Be careful about what you put on paper. Paper can be subpoenaed.
- Be VERY careful what you write in email or say on a voice mail. Be careful when sharing information from the internet. If written on a school computer, it is archived and can be undeleted. Voicemail can be forwarded. This information can be subpoenaed.

Data Collection Form 1 – Elementary

Student Initials:		Date:	Grade:
Classroom teacher:			

How was the student's day?	☺ ☺ ☹ Other?

Time	Grouping (circle)	Student Behavior (How did he/she do?)	Activity	✓
	I S W		Phonics/Phonemic Awareness	
	I S W		Word Identification	
	I S W		Comprehension	
	I S W		Vocabulary (meaning emphasis)	
	I S W		Spelling/Mechanics	
	I S W		Oral Language	
	I S W		Reading: Choral, Guided, Partner, Independent	
	I S W		Math: Computation, Organization	
	I S W			
	I S W			

I – Individual   S – Small Group   W – Whole Class

When was the student engaged or not engaged in the class activities? What worked?	
What supplemental materials worked?	
How did the student engage with peers?	
How did the student respond to testing situations?	
How did the student do during unstructured time? (Recess, Hall, Cafeteria, etc.)	

Data Collection Form 2 – Secondary

Student Initials:		Date:	Grade:
Classroom teacher:			

How was the student's day?	☺ ☺ ☹ Other?

Time	Grouping (circle)	Student Behavior (How did he/she do?)	Activity	✓
	I S W		Phonics/Phonemic Awareness	
	I S W		Word Identification	
	I S W		Comprehension	
	I S W		Vocabulary (meaning emphasis)	
	I S W		Spelling/Mechanics	
	I S W		Oral Language	
	I S W		Reading: Choral, Guided, Partner, Independent	
	I S W		Math: Computation, Organization	
	I S W			
	I S W			

I – Individual   S – Small Group   W – Whole Class

When was the student engaged or not engaged in the class activities? What worked?	
What adaptations worked?	
How did the student respond to testing situations?	
How did the student do during unstructured time?	
General Behavioral Comments	

Differentiating Roles-A Legal Priority

What is the teacher's role? What is the paraprofessional's role? It is critical that the supervising teacher, the paraprofessional, and, when appropriate, the special educator clearly define classroom roles. Some responsibilities should not be assigned to paraprofessionals. Tasks that could pose legal or safety threats to the paraprofessional, that violate union rules, or tasks that are not appropriate or fair are examples of such responsibilities.

Should a paraprofessional be left alone in the classroom? This dilemma challenges most schools and districts given the shortage of substitute teachers. There have been times when I have had a paraprofessional in the classroom and I needed to slip out for a valid reason and the paraprofessional covered my class. This, however, is rarely part of a paraprofessional's job description. Regardless, it sometimes happens in the real world. It is important to be aware and knowledgeable of the paraprofessional's role and to make sure paraprofessionals are not put in positions where they might be liable for more than what is legally or contractually appropriate. The paraprofessional should not be responsible for the classroom if the supervising teacher is absent.

Because paraprofessionals were often more knowledgeable and better equipped to manage the class in my absence, when I needed to be out for a day, a substitute teacher would often follow my paraprofessional's lead. The district eventually "hired" paraprofessionals as the substitute teacher with the pay and protections one gets with that job. The paraprofessional was under a substitute contract for a day. This option might work in some schools; however, it is important that this option be exercised within the rules of the state and within the guidelines for the district.

In addition, the paraprofessional should never be responsible for designing curriculum or modifying content. For example, a reduction of content is not appropriate, unless the paraprofessional has been authorized to make that modification based on IEP requirements and the recommendation of the general educator and the special education teacher. Paraprofessionals are not responsible for creating lesson plans or providing initial instruction for students.

Paraprofessionals may provide additional reinforcement, may create adaptations and activities that enhance learning, memory, and recall.

Concerns on Which to Reach Agreement

In order to have a more harmonious and effective working relationship in the classroom, it is important to be on the same page with matters of concern in the classroom. Consider discussing how the paraprofessional will plan for his or her work in the classroom. Other items to consider include "How will the paraprofessional meet instructional goals? What are the teacher's expectations for participation in classroom management? How will the classroom teacher and paraprofessional communicate with each other?"

Lesson Planning

- Will the paraprofessional provide input into the planning process for either specific students or the class in general? If so, how will the classroom teacher gain that input?
- Will the paraprofessional have input into lesson planning or planning for re-teaching?
- When and how should the paraprofessional's experience in the classroom contribute to interventions used with non-responders or students with special needs?

Instruction

- With whom will the paraprofessional work: students with special needs, non-responders, students at risk, or the general student population?
- Will the paraprofessional re-teach material?
- When and how will the need for re-teaching be decided?
- How will the paraprofessional help implement lesson plans or provide re-teaching? What will this look like?
- If specific interventions or programs are being utilized, who will train the paraprofessional in these methods?
- When will student assessment take place? How will gains be recorded? Who will be responsible for collecting this data?

Student Behavior

- What are the behavioral expectations and rules for students in the classroom?
- What methods are used to gain student understanding of classroom expectations and rules?
- How will students perceive those expectations and rules in regards to the paraprofessional's authority? Who clarifies the paraprofessional's level of authority?
- How should the paraprofessional deal with misbehavior, disruptions, or problems that occur in the classroom?
- Who will provide the paraprofessional with positive behavior management training when necessary?

Communication

- How and when will professionals and paraprofessionals communicate about concerns, student updates, intervention progress, etc.?
- Who will be responsible for communicating with parents?
- Will communication with parents be verbal or written? What parameters should the paraprofessional work within? Are there times when communication should be deferred to the classroom teacher, special educator, or administrator?
- When should conversations with parents be documented? When should they not be documented?
- If documented, what form should that documentation take?
- Exactly who should the paraprofessional report to if any conversation with a parent occurs that might cause concerns, or where student issues need to be related?

The Daily Schedule

Once you have defined your roles in the classroom, the next step is to determine a manageable schedule. This schedule will vary from paraprofessional to paraprofessional depending upon:

- The grade level in which the paraprofessional is working.
- Whether the paraprofessional is a one-on-one student assistant.
- Whether the paraprofessional is working with an entire class to support students on an IEP.
- Whether the paraprofessional is in a secondary education situation, working with various teachers in various subjects over the course of a school day and supporting any number of students with special needs.

The paraprofessional and the general education teacher need time to sit down and communicate what this schedule shall look like.

Scheduling in the Elementary School

At the elementary level, it is important to prepare a schedule collaboratively that addresses:

- The teacher's classroom goals and schedule for the day.
- The assignments, activities, and tasks that the teacher intends to instruct over the course of the day.
- Areas in which the student or students may need assistance.
- Areas in which the teacher may need support in meeting student needs.

Scheduling at the Secondary Level

At the secondary level, the paraprofessional often moves between several classes during the course of a school day.

In the role of a one-on-one student assistant, the paraprofessional will follow the student through most periods of the school day, with the exception of the paraprofessional's own lunchtime. In a one-on-one position, the student's specific needs might be the most critical factor in determining how time is scheduled in each one of those classes. When paraprofessionals are moving between classes it is more challenging to make time for collaboration between the general education teacher and the paraprofessional to sort out this schedule.

The benefits, however, of investing time in designing a meaningful schedule, whether it be before class starts, at the beginning of the week, or at the beginning of a unit of instruction, are that the paraprofessional will be able to:

- Assist the teacher more effectively
- Schedule times for the student to be independent in his or her work situation
- Ensure that there are social interactions so that the student grows emotionally and socially
- Coordinate activities so that things run smoothly

Other times, the paraprofessional may be working with a variety of students over the course of the school day, serving the needs of several students on an IEP in the class. The paraprofessional is often working with many different teachers, and thus personalities, over the course of each day. Each teacher will have his or her own scheduling concerns, priorities, and needs. It is important that these scheduling issues within the class period are discussed and worked out so that everyone wins.

How do you go about managing both the time for communication and the schedule? Use the checklists and forms included in this section as guides to decide the different aspects of the paraprofessional's role in the classroom. This step is critical to scheduling time.

Once a schedule is set, there are still times when a paraprofessional may feel that his or her time is not well spent. If the paraprofessional feels that time is being wasted, or that his or her professional skills are not being used, he or she may use this time to perform other activities that can support classroom goals. Refer back to Paraprofessional roles or jobs for suggestions on how to maximize class time, or consider the following options:

- Start to accumulate a binder of the course content for the students to match up their work against.
- Observe a student or collect behavioral data.
- Write down comments or discussion items to review collaboratively with the classroom teacher or special educator.
- Move about the room and use position control to make sure students in the class are on task, understanding their work, or behaving appropriately.
- Consider the concepts being taught in the classroom at that time and think of reinforcement activities for memorization and recall, review and practice, or re-teaching that could benefit students on an IEP and possibly all students in the class.

Sample Secondary Level Daily Schedule – Multiple Locations

Time	Location	Subject	Support Function	Supervising Teacher
8:30-8:40	Front Foyer	N/A	Pick up student from bus	N/A
8:45-9:30	Hall B Room 23	Language Arts	Inclusion Classroom – Re-teach, read aloud with students	J. Smith
9:25-10:35	Hall C Room 14	Social Studies	One-on-one assist for M. T.	H. Gingras
10:40-11:25	Hall B Room 24	Language Arts	Inclusion Classroom – Re-teach, read aloud with students	J. Smith
11:30-12:15	Lunch			
12:20-1:05	Hall C Room 18	Social Studies	Inclusion Classroom – Provide small group and individual support as needed.	E. Sanchez
1:10-1:55	Resource Room	N/A	Provide tutorial support. Re-teach study skills. Drill and reinforcement.	R. Littledove
2:00-2:50	Hall B Room 23	Language Arts	Inclusion Classroom – Re-teach, read aloud with students	J. Smith

Secondary Level Daily Schedule – Multiple Locations

Time	Location	Subject	Support Function	Supervising Teacher

Sample Elementary Level Daily Schedule – Single Location

Time	Subject	Support Function	Notes
8:30-8:40	N/A	Pick up student from bus	
8:45-10:00	Reading	Re-teach, read aloud with students	
10:00-10:15	Recess	Supervise on the playground	
10:15-11:25	Language Arts	Re-teach, lead small group	
11:30-12:00	Lunch		
12:00-12:40	Specials	Inclusion Classroom – Provide small group and individual supports as needed.	
12:40-1:00	Science	Provide tutorial support. Re-teach study skills. Drill and reinforcement.	
2:00-2:50	Social Studies	Re-teach, read aloud with students, play review game	
2:50-3:15	Dismissal Routines	Engage students in activities while waiting to be called for dismissal	

Elementary Level Daily Schedule —Single Location

Time	Subject	Support Function	Notes

How Do I Follow-Up Outside of Class?

Sample Letters to Assist With Follow-Up

Secondary Level

The following letters are helpful for paraprofessionals working within an academic support class environment. Often students come to the class without their work. Gathering information about missing assignments helps the paraprofessional work more effectively with students.

Date:

Dear (Teacher's name),

(Student's name) is in (Study Hall, Resource Room, Support Lab, etc.) _____ class period. Would you please let me know if there is work missing or due for your class? It will assist me greatly in helping him/her to be successful in your class. If you feel that this student could benefit from any ongoing re-teaching, that information would be helpful as well. I appreciate your assistance.

Sincerely,

(Paraprofessional's name)

Date:

Dear (Teacher's name),

(Student's name) is in your _____ period class, and has (Study Hall, Resource Room, Support Lab, etc.) _____ class period. If you could take a moment to fill out the information below it will assist me greatly in helping this student succeed in your class.

Please Circle One:
1. Estimate Grade: A   B   C   D   F
2. Turns in Homework: Always   Sometimes   Never
3. Tests/Quizzes: High   Average   Low   Failing
4. Do you feel this student could benefit from any ongoing re-teaching activities?   Yes   No

If Yes, please explain.

5. Is this student missing any assignments/tests that need to be made up/completed?   Yes   No

If Yes, please provide details.

Thank you for taking the time to complete this form!

Sincerely,

(Paraprofessional's name)

Date:

Dear (Teacher's name),

The following students are in your _____ period class and have (Resource Room, Study Skills, Study Support, etc.). If you could take a moment to fill out the form below, it would assist me greatly in helping these students succeed in your class.

Please return to (Paraprofessional's name) by (date).

Student Name	Est. Grade	Missing Homework?	Missing Tests/Quizzes?	Assignments/Tests that need to be made up or completed	Comments

Thank you for taking the time to complete this form!

Sincerely,

(Paraprofessional's name)

Keeping Up With the IEP

Class List Adaptations Chart

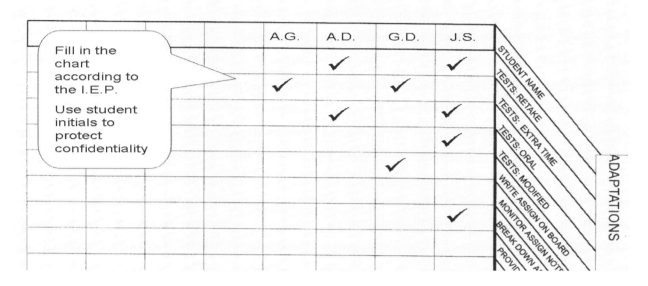

The class list adaptations chart enables teachers and paraprofessionals to remember IEP adaptations with a class snapshot.

The "one sheet at a glance" adaptation list is a quick way to keep track of IEP modifications and student considerations. It does _not_ replace reading the IEP.
- Place the names of the students who have IEPs across the top of the chart.
- Check off the adaptations in the column under the students' names.
- Code special considerations as necessary.
- Reference this list before testing, assigning projects, and as a daily reminder.

See the next page for another version of this form.

Adaptations and Learning Profile - One Page View

						⟲ Student Initials/⟳Information
						Tests: Retake
						Tests: Extra Time
						Tests: Oral
						Tests: Modified
						Tests: Scribe
						Write Assignments on Board
						Monitor Assignment Notebook
						Break Down Assignments into Steps
						Provide Copies of Notes
						Substitute Hands-on for Written
						Substitute Oral for Written
						Seating Preference
						Allow Word Processor
						Allow Calculator
						Allow Text to Speech Software
						Allow Speech to Text Software
						Provide Advanced Organizer
						Needs One-to-One Assistance
						Visual Cues & Hands-on Critical
						Easily Overwhelmed
						Distractible
						Written Expression Weak
						Verbal Expression Weak
						Auditory Learner
						Visual Learner
						Kinesthetic Learner

Download a .pdf or .doc version of this form at www.aimhieducational.com/inclusion.aspx.
Click on the "Differentiating Instructions, IEP Adaptations & Gifted" tab.

IEP-Based Planning Forms

CONFIDENTIAL

Student		Grade Level

Learning Style	Multiple Intelligence

Interests

Strengths	Challenges

Notes/Reminders:

Areas of Concern:

Class Activity	Adapted Student Activity	IEP Reference	Additional Supports Needed

Other:

Part 2: Collaboration

A Paraprofessional's Point of View

Teamwork between the paraprofessional and the classroom teacher is an essential ingredient to a successful inclusion classroom. When a paraprofessional is assigned to a class, he or she should be seen as a part of the solution and not as an intrusion. Ideally, the paraprofessional and the classroom teacher have some common planning time to discuss upcoming assignments, progress of students, and methods to help the students succeed. Without this time, it is difficult to establish a strong working relationship; however, the relationship can still be beneficial.

Paraprofessionals can be valuable resources in the classroom. They can work in class with students who are having difficulty understanding the information, provide notes for those students who are unable to take comprehensive notes during class time, and provide help with test and assignment modifications for students with learning disabilities.

Student follow-up is especially important to meet IEP requirements and promote success. Often, the paraprofessional can follow up in the resource room as well as in class. Paraprofessionals can support the classroom teacher by answering the questions of all students.

Paraprofessionals are an integral and important part of the classroom team. They are happy to contribute whatever they can to add to the success of all the students. If the teacher is accepting of the paraprofessional's presence, then the students will also accept it as normal and will consider him or her as the extra, valuable resource he or she is.

Ginger Davis
Londonderry High School

Potential Roadblocks: Differences

What are some of the problems, or obstacles, that come up between the paraprofessional and the classroom teacher that make it difficult to work together?

Teaching (and Re-teaching) Methodology

One roadblock often evolves from a difference in how both approach teaching. One might think this would not be an issue for the paraprofessional as it sometimes is for the co-teacher; however, it is a problem when the personalities clash in the way a classroom is run, or if the way a paraprofessional re-teaches or manages students within the classroom does not sit well with the teacher's personality style.

Personality Differences

For example, Bob, who was working with several different teachers through the course of the day, was exasperated because, in his opinion, one of the classrooms he was working with was totally out of control. The teacher had a more loosely structured style of managing the classroom than was Bob's preference. Bob preferred a structured and ordered room where kids worked quietly, were orderly, did not speak out, and essentially were what we would expect from a traditional classroom: well-behaved.

The loose structure of the classroom, however, made it less likely that students would be quiet or stay in their seats for any length of time. This drove Bob crazy. It created stress and conflict because he felt powerless in his position to do anything about it.

Following is another example of a situation that is potentially a conflict. A classroom teacher with very unequivocal ideas about how teaching should happen in the classroom and what help a student should or should not get is paired with a paraprofessional who will do anything and everything he or she can do to get students to do the work. That might include cajoling, bribing, doing half of the work for them, talking to students (while the teacher is presenting) to try to convince them to get work done, etc.

There are potential problems in either scenario, but when the two adults in the room are so very different in their approach to teaching, or re-teaching, it is difficult to find a balance. Communication is the best solution. The paraprofessional, however, does not often feel confident in his or her ability to have that conversation because he or she often concludes, "It is not my class, so I cannot say anything about it."

Comfort Zones

Comfort zones are another significant factor in whether a relationship will be compatible. Many times, we are asked to do things in the classroom that are outside the comfort zone of either the teacher or the paraprofessional in the classroom. Possibly the IEP requires the paraprofessional or the classroom teacher to use strategies that are unusual or unfamiliar. Or perhaps one of the two adults may not be comfortable having another adult in the room. On the other hand, given professional differences, one may not be comfortable being the other person in the classroom. When we are out of our comfort zones, we struggle.

Legal Worries

Often, the general education teacher is concerned about not meeting the educational needs of students with disabilities or the IEP requirements adequately. This is especially true when students have significant disabilities or physical disabilities. This can create a roadblock because the paraprofessional may become the sole provider of all teaching and assistance for that student, or may even be the sole source of communication for that student.

Sometimes the teacher will feel more comfortable saying, "You take care of Johnny, because you know how to deal with Johnny and I don't. I'm not a special education teacher." This is caused by a concern that he cannot meet the student's needs or that legally he could get into trouble if he takes responsibility and then cannot meet that responsibility according to the standards of the law. This belief often feeds into the attitude of "Those sped kids are yours."

Even if the paraprofessional is a one-to-one assistant in the classroom, the general education teacher is ultimately responsible for the education of the child. This is especially an issue with the current mandate of No Child Left Behind.

This Is Not the Way It Should Be

Another area of conflict and another roadblock to overcome when two adults work in a classroom together is differences in teaching styles. Often both enter the room with specific ideas of how the class should operate and how things should be. However, there is often a misperception about what is happening in the classroom, especially in the case where there has been little to no communication between these two adults prior to the first day of classes. Moreover, if class is not proceeding the way one or both of them thinks that it should, there is a problem. Again, communication is paramount in this situation. Communication simply must happen.

Feelings of Intimidation

At times, a general classroom teacher may be intimidated by a paraprofessional with a strong personality in the classroom. However, more often the paraprofessional is the one who feels intimidated in that situation because of the potentially powerless position he or she holds. Communication can help to alleviate concerns that may arise regarding feelings of intimidation.

In my role as a consultant, I have often heard paraprofessionals share stories of their unhappiness in the classroom and their unwillingness to communicate with the classroom teacher about their concerns. The classroom teacher can help with this situation immensely by periodically asking the paraprofessional how he or she is doing. Asking paraprofessionals if they are they getting what they need, or how things could work better in the classroom for both the paraprofessional and the student with special needs, simply creates opportunities for more comfortable communication.

By being proactive, the general education teacher can minimize the amount of conflict in the classroom and increase the efficacy of the working relationship by simply checking in with their paraprofessionals on a regular basis. This does not need to be an hour-long meeting. This can be done in two minutes here, three minutes there, or while passing in the hall and chatting for a few minutes; whatever it takes. It is worth the investment in time. It is worth asking.

Credibility

Another roadblock that frequently comes up when general education teachers are working with paraprofessionals is one of credibility. Often a paraprofessional is thrown into the classroom without any training. Unfortunately, the classroom teacher may not even be aware of the paraprofessional's strengths or areas of expertise, his or her background, or ability to meet the requirements of the job.

The classroom teacher needs and wants a paraprofessional who can simply come in and do the job well. Unfortunately, this does not always happen. The key to this dilemma is training. The classroom teacher or the special educator needs to take the time to share expectations with the paraprofessional, to explain the teaching methods being used, and to teach the paraprofessional how to use those methods.

Insufficient Time

If I have heard it once, I have heard it 100 times: there is simply not enough time to prepare materials for students, to meet with the teacher to learn strategies, or to get anything done proactively for the classroom. So often, paraprofessionals are sent from room to room with barely enough time to eat lunch or take care of their personal needs.

If we want paraprofessionals to be effective with students with special needs in the classroom, we need to change our paradigms about planning and prep time. Districts need to take into consideration the time that paraprofessionals need to have in order to gain the skills we expect them to acquire for working with our students' special needs.

Some districts address this issue by holding monthly trainings for paraprofessionals within the school day. Paraprofessionals are released from their responsibilities for one or two hours of the school day to attend training. The training can be led by a master teacher or experienced paraprofessional so that bringing someone in from the outside is not always necessary. This practice enables new and less experienced paraprofessionals to gain knowledge during the workday.

In the situation of a one-to-one assistant, release time may be more difficult to accomplish. Creative solutions may need to be considered. It is possible that a substitute who has the same period free will be able to cover for that paraprofessional. Alternatively, maybe another adult in the building would be willing to cover.

There are solutions to almost every issue, and those solutions are worth looking into, especially when finding the solution means that the paraprofessional will have the skills to be more successful in the classroom, with students overall, and in their relationships with the classroom teacher.

Lack of Administrative Support

Administrative support can also be a roadblock to the success of the paraprofessional working in the general education classroom. Sometimes this is simply because administrators have been unable or unwilling to provide paraprofessionals with training, time to communicate with their teachers, or even time to prep re-teaching materials. Funding can be an obstacle if there are limited monies available to provide quality training and follow-up. At times, there is a lack of support for inclusion efforts and for implementing the differentiated instruction necessary to meet the goals of No Child Left Behind. Other times, an administrator may simply have no voice amongst teachers to say loud and clear, "This is a legal requirement. We need to do it and you are accountable."

Potential Roadblocks: Other Practicalities

- At times, there is insufficient time & flexibility.
- It can be difficult to see lesson plans ahead of class time.
- There is often a lack of training in a problem-solving approach to collaboration.
- Cost of training and staffing minimizes available opportunities for professional development.
- What might you add?

Overcoming Roadblocks: Solutions

Be Flexible

Foremost, flexibility is a necessary trait for the paraprofessional. It is also an important quality for the general education teacher in an inclusive classroom. This can be a difficult requirement because our personalities are not always innately flexible. Some of us find it easier to go with the flow and take things as they come or to let things roll off our backs than others do. In the working relationship between a paraprofessional and teacher, without flexibility, there is rigidity. With rigidity, there is often a strained relationship. Be flexible and life will be easier and your students will be better served.

Identify and Focus on Your Paraprofessional's Strengths

The teacher has strengths in the classroom. The paraprofessional also has strengths. Find those strengths and celebrate them. This may be one of the most viable solutions to lack of training. If we find our strong points, we can work with those assets without requiring additional training. It is a logical solution to a common difficulty.

Adopt a "They are all our students" Attitude

This is not only critical for the paraprofessional, but also extremely important for the students with special needs within the classroom. It is especially important to work with students in the general classroom in such a way that students with special needs are not stigmatized. Stigmatization as a "sped kid" leaves scars that can last a lifetime.

When the paraprofessional takes on the ownership of a student and the general classroom teacher leaves all interactions for that student to the paraprofessional, everyone loses. The teacher does not develop a potentially rewarding relationship with the student. The student becomes overly dependent upon the paraprofessional, having less social interaction with other students and less interaction with another adult. The student with special needs knows he or she is being ignored or left out by the general education teacher, which reinforces feelings of inferiority.

Overcoming Roadblocks: Summary & More

- Be flexible
- Identify and focus on teacher/paraprofessional strengths
- Adopt a "They are all OUR students" attitude
- Be self-aware
- Assess your viewpoints of the teaching profession
- Reflect on past experiences with change
- Understand your stage of life and career goals
- Consider gender and culture's impact on the relationship between you and the other adult in the classroom
- What is the perception of particular change being considered?
- Increase your understanding of personality types

Perceptions & Personality

Looking at Personality Types

One of the most difficult aspects of working in the classroom with another adult is navigating personalities. Any time we work in a classroom, whether because of the personality of the students or the personality of the adults, we will face challenges due to our differences. It is important to understand your students' personalities and how their personalities influence their learning styles. When we understand learning style, we can be more helpful to our students by teaching them to identify how they learn and enabling them to learn to their maximum capability using strategies that fit their learning style.

Most of us realize the importance of understanding student learning styles, and possibly even understand the importance of having an awareness of different personalities. However, this aspect of relationships is often glossed over or completely ignored in school environments.

In industry, managers, human resource departments, trainers, and team builders commonly understand the importance of understanding personality types. Sometimes businesses will even group people based on the best fit between different personalities. Schools have a tendency to simply throw people together and expect them to figure out how to collaborate and work together with virtually no training or insight into personality theory, group process, or negotiation.

When I started working with other teachers in the classroom, I quickly discovered that one of the most critical lessons I needed to learn was to understand personality styles. What was most critical was understanding my own personality and how my personality affected others.

When I spoke with my 'demonstrative body language,' with every bit of 'passion' that I shared, with my 'extraversion' emphasizing every aspect of who I was, I intimidated people or overwhelmed some without even knowing it. It became clear to me that without an understanding of personality, I would continue to have relationships in the classroom that were not as productive as they could be. Too much time was spent misinterpreting each other, misunderstanding motivation, and sometimes taking those misunderstandings much too personally.

Working with the paraprofessional in the classroom requires the same amount of understanding and insight about personality. Everyone is different; some people approach the world from a logical standpoint, whereas some people approach the world from a values and harmony standpoint. Some people think and then speak. Some people speak and then think. Some need closure and make quick decisions; others want to keep their possibilities open. It helps when we understand personalities.

Let us look at some personalities that we might work with in the classroom. Here are some vignettes from my own experience.

(Names of the following personalities are changed to protect confidentiality.)

Meet Elaina
Elaina is a strong woman who exudes confidence and knows exactly what she believes in. Elaina works with students in the classroom as if it is her personal mission in life. She keeps up with each student and knows everything he or she is required to do. She does this completely without being told how or when to follow up. Elaina's organizational skills put everyone else to shame. She keeps a binder for every classroom in which she works. These big, blue binders have dividers for every bit of notes, every test, and every piece of information students are required to have. She keeps notes on the students regarding their IEP goals and requirements. She also keeps a sample binder against which her students can check their work. She leaves these binders – minus the confidential information – in a public place so that people can access them and benefit from them. Elaina does not hesitate to tell anyone she works with exactly how she feels about a situation. If she is offended, you will know it. If she likes you, you will know it. In addition, she will not take any excuses from anyone, especially the students. Elaina is caring, strong, and passionate.

Meet Kay
Kay is quiet and a bit timid. Kay comes into the classroom silently, sits down, and scopes out the room. When she sees that a student might need help, Kay will discretely move over to that student's side of the room and, in a voice that is barely discernible, she will begin to tutor that student. She carries herself with elegance and exudes the utmost respect and dignity in everything she does. Kay knows her material and gets work done, but she will not deal with complex issues. If there are behavioral issues in the classroom, Kay will wait for the classroom teacher to manage it or she will ignore it. Kay cares deeply about her students; however, she is uncomfortable in the role of a disciplinarian.

Meet Maggie

Maggie has been working many years as a paraprofessional. Maggie's own children had learning challenges, so she has navigated the system from the viewpoint of a parent, not just from the perspective of a paraprofessional. She understands her students and the teachers she is working with. She manages to find a way to tell people exactly what she thinks and communicates what she needs in a manner that is never offensive, always loving, and is simply amenable. Maggie knows exactly when someone needs a perk and will share a little card, a thank you, a small gift, or a piece of chocolate with whomever she works. Maggie is a leader that takes initiative.

Meet Ellen

Ellen is new in her position. Ellen has not worked closely with children before with the exception of her own. She cares deeply, but feels a little uncomfortable in the teacher's classroom. She is unsure of what to do and when to do it because she is extremely concerned about offending the teacher or doing something wrong. She is bothered by classroom disruption. Rude students offend her, yet her big heart pushes her to continue to strive, learning to help the students and the teachers in the classroom. Ellen needs to be told what to do every step of the way. When she understands her instructions, she does them willingly and the work is outstanding. Ellen needs some help learning teaching strategies. When watching Ellen give a test, sometimes it seems she gives just a little bit too much help. Ellen wants her students to succeed so badly that sometimes she does a little bit too much of the work for them.

Personality Preference and Learning Style

The MBTI®, Myers-Briggs Type Indicator® personality inventory, reports a person's preferred way of 'being' in the world and his or her preferred process for making decisions.

Characteristics of Personality Type (Myers-Briggs)

- There are polar opposites for each preference, and each is useful and important.
- Your preferences for certain mental habits are a persistent part of your personality.
- There are no good or bad types.
- Psychological type is not an intelligence test.
- Everyone is an individual; type only helps us understand part of our personality (and learning style).
- The MBTI is an indicator. It indicates preference. It is not a test.
- Following is a description of the four scales reported in the MBTI and several teaching approaches that will appeal to different MBTI profiles.

Extraversion (E) versus Introversion (I)

This preference tells us how people "get their energy."
- *Extraverts* find energy in things and people. They prefer interaction with others, and are action-oriented. Extraverts are spontaneous thinkers who talk their thoughts aloud. Their motto is: Ready, Fire, Aim. For the extravert, there is no impression without expression.
- *Introverts* find energy in the inner world of ideas, concepts, and abstractions. They can be sociable, but need quiet to recharge their batteries. Introverts want to understand the world. Introverts concentrate and reflect. Their motto is: Ready, Aim, Aim... For the introvert, there is no impression without reflection.

> "If you don't know what an extravert is thinking, you haven't been listening. But, if you don't know what an introvert is thinking, you haven't asked!"

Sensing (S) versus Intuition (N)

This preference tells us how people take in information.
- *Sensing* types rely on their five senses. Sensing people are detail-oriented; they want facts and trust those facts.
- *Intuition* types rely on their imagination and what can be seen in "the mind's eye." Intuitive people seek out patterns and relationships among the facts they have gathered. They trust hunches and their intuition and look for the "big picture."

> "Sensing types help intuitives keep their heads out of the clouds,
> while intuitives help sensing types keep their heads out of a rut."

Thinking (T) versus Feeling (F)

This preference tells us how people make decisions.
- *Thinking* types prefer to decide things impersonally based on analysis, logic, and principle. Thinking students value fairness. What could be fairer than focusing on the situation's logic, and placing great weight on objective criteria in making a decision?
- *Feeling* types prefer to make decisions by focusing on human values. Feeling students value harmony. They focus on human values and needs as they make decisions or arrive at judgments. They tend to be good at persuasion and easing differences among group members.

> "Thinking types need to remember that feelings are also facts that they need to consider,
> while feeling types need to remember that thinking types have feelings too!"

Judging (J) versus Perceptive (P)

This preference tells us people's attitudes toward the outside world.
- *Judging* types prefer to make quick decisions. Judging people are decisive, planful (they make plans), and self-regimented. They focus on completing the task, only want to know the essentials, and take action quickly (perhaps too quickly). They plan their work and work their plan. Deadlines are sacred. Their motto is: Just do it!
- *Perceptive* types prefer to postpone action and seek more data. Perceptive people are curious, adaptable, and spontaneous. They start many tasks, want to know everything about each task, and often find it difficult to complete a task. Deadlines are meant to be stretched. Their motto is: On the other hand...

> "Judging types can help perceiving types meet deadlines,
> while perceiving types can help keep judging types open to new information."

MBTI Self Assessment Table

Jung's Preference Types

Worksheet

E – Extroversion			Introversion - I
Energized by outer world			Energized by inner world

S – Sensing			Intuition - N
Work with known facts			Look for possibilities and relationships

T – Thinking			Feeling - F
Base decisions on impersonal analysis and logic			Base decisions on personal values

J – Judging			Perceiving - P
Prefer a planned, decided, orderly way of life			Prefer a flexible, spontaneous way of life

Very Clear Clear Moderate Slight | Slight Moderate Clear Very Clear

	E or I	S or N	T or F	J or P
Self Assessment Type				
Indicator Type				

After reading the previous pages, use this form to mark your preferences. What type do you think you are? What type does the Myers-Brigg's Indicator state as your preference? Is your preference in each function clear or slight?

If you have the opportunity to take the MBTI inventory, fill those preferences in the bottom row. Is there a difference between your self-assessment type and your MBTI inventory results? If there is, simply read descriptions of your

Myers-Briggs preferences according to your self-assessed report and your Indicator reports. Which one fits your personality more? The MBTI inventory simply indicates your preferences. Only you can decide your personality type.

Remember, these results are not carved in stone. Use this information as a launching board to discovering your type and gaining a deeper understanding of yourself and others.

The MBTI Type Table

ISTJ	ISFJ	INFJ	INTJ
ISTP	ISFP	INFP	INTP
ESTP	ESFP	ENFP	ENTP
ESTJ	ESFJ	ENFJ	ENTJ

The following chart, "Tip Sheet: How to communicate with…" may be used to determine how you might communicate with another personality type. For example, if you want to present a proposal to an INTJ, then you would be more successful in convincing the INTJ to accept the proposal if you:

- Give them time to process and reflect on what you are proposing.
- Develop alternative solutions rather than presenting just one option.
- Present information to INTJ with logic.
- Ensure closure. INTJ needs a decision; to leave without setting up a date to reach closure would be problematic for INTJ.
- Demonstrate your knowledge, competency, and credibility when presenting the proposal.

MBTI Tip Sheet: How to communicate with…

ISTJ	ISFJ	INFJ	INTJ
• Give them time to process & reflect • Know & present the facts • Present information with logic • Ensure closure – needs a decision • Present measured results & data	• Give them time to process & reflect • Know & present the facts • Understand people values • Ensure closure – needs a decision • Point out practical benefits	• Give them time to process & reflect • Develop alternative solutions • Understand people values • Ensure closure – needs a decision • Point out value to relationships	• Give them time to process & reflect • Develop alternative solutions • Present information with logic • Ensure closure – needs a decision • Demonstrate competency
ISTP	**ISFP**	**INFP**	**INTP**
• Give them time to process & reflect • Know & present the facts • Present information with logic • Be flexible • Present measured results & data	• Give them time to process & reflect • Know & present the facts • Understand people values • Be flexible • Point out practical benefits	• Give them time to process & reflect • Develop alternative solutions • Understand people values • Be flexible • Point out value to relationships	• Give them time to process & reflect • Develop alternative solutions • Present information with logic • Be flexible • Demonstrate competency
ESTP	**ESFP**	**ENFP**	**ENTP**
• Put agreements into words • Know & present the facts • Present information with logic • Be flexible • Present measured results & data	• Put agreements into words • Know & present the facts • Understand people values • Be flexible • Point out practical benefits	• Put agreements into words • Develop alternative solutions • Understand people values • Be flexible • Point out value to relationships	• Put agreements into words • Develop alternative solutions • Present information with logic • Be flexible • Demonstrate competence
ESTJ	**ESFJ**	**ENFJ**	**ENTJ**
• Put agreements into words • Know & present the facts • Present information with logic • Ensure closure – needs a decision • Present measured results & data	• Put agreements into words • Know & present the facts • Understand people values • Ensure closure – needs a decision • Point out practical benefits	• Put agreements into words • Develop alternative solutions • Understand people values • Ensure closure – needs a decision • Point out value to relationships	• Put agreements into words • Develop alternative solutions • Present information with logic • Ensure closure – needs a decision • Demonstrate competency

*The author of the chart "Tip Sheet: How to communicate with…" is unknown.

When in Conflict

There are times in the classroom when there will be a conflict with the teacher with whom one is working. Alternatively, there will be times when a classroom teacher will have a problem or a conflict with a paraprofessional. How does a person handle that conflict in a constructive way? How does a person manage the relationship so that both can work together without offending or hurting each other? When situations get tough, one of the first things to remember is that when in conflict, it is most often about personality. That other person is not trying to get you.

What are we thinking when something happens in the classroom that triggers our frustration or our anger? Often we are thinking such things as, "That person should know better," or "I told her that she should do such and such, and she didn't listen to me!" or "Every time this happens in the classroom, she does that simply to annoy me." "She's an idiot." "He thinks he knows everything!" "He is a control freak. I can't stand him." Every one of these types of statements that we think to ourselves in times of conflict is negative self-talk. Negative self-talk begets more negativity, anger, frustration, and dissatisfaction.

What if we change our self-talk? What if, instead of saying, "This person is doing this to annoy me," we replaced that thought with, "She's trying her best. This is just her personality. How might I approach this personality that is so different from me in her approach to the world?" What if we simply say, "I can handle this," or, "This isn't about me, this is about him, and I need to know how to approach him."

When we can take a step back and look at this situation in terms of personality, it is much easier to handle conflicts in the classroom. Instead of taking things personally, we understand that it is simply about personality and a person's comfort level.

Once you have your positive self-talk – for example, you have told yourself, "I can handle this!" – start considering solutions to the problem. Seek the consult of a respected colleague, or someone you know who really understands how to approach different personalities. You will find that person by looking for someone who seems to be able to work with just about anyone and who has an amazing understanding of people. Seek that person out and ask him or her how you might approach the problem. Ideally, you would do this without naming the person with whom you are having a problem.

There are many resources available to help people figure out what to say. In a difficult situation, use these resources. Albert Ellis has several books on the market that share strategies for handling difficult situations and feelings and suggesting ways to keep our minds in a rational and positive place. For example, just the title of his book, *"How to Stubbornly Refuse to Make Yourself Miserable About Anything – Yes, Anything"* (Paperback - July 1988) encourages a smile.

Consider using "I" statements to share how you feel about a situation. Avoid using the word "you" when communicating how you feel. Be careful to avoid blaming language. Even if you believe the other person is wrong, find a way to approach the conversation from a positive perspective. Once you figure out how you want to handle the problem, role-play a conversation with another trusted colleague or friend. Visualize the interaction in your mind. Practice what you will say until you feel confident. Visualize that you are successful in this interaction.

There are times when it is best to say nothing. That choice is more difficult for some personalities than for others. There are times it is important to speak up about our concerns, and that is easier for some personalities and more difficult for others. The most critical factor is that whatever we choose to do, we try to frame our actions, our words, and our thoughts in positive ways.

When In Conflict

- Change negative self-talk to positive
- Consider "Next time X happens... I'll do Y or Z"
- Plan viable solutions
- Consider personality type
- Seek suggestions from a supportive colleague or read Albert Ellis for suggestions to reframe
- Visualize yourself in the interaction ***BEING SUCCESSSFUL!***
- Affirm: "I CAN handle this situation"

Stopping Conflict In Its Tracks!

Have you ever had people in your life who seem to enjoy baiting you? Have you wondered if all of their amusement in life comes from trying to get a rise out of you? Have you ever found yourself in a conversation with a colleague, and, when the conversation finished, shaking your head and asking yourself, "What was that all about?" Have you ever thought, "I should have said this!" and "I should have said that!" Often we leave the conversations feeling defeated, and strangely so, because we are not always sure what happened.

Do you have someone you interact with who seems to have an answer for everything? What about someone who happens to be overly critical? How do we handle these types of conversations and these characters in our lives who challenge us with their words? Consider learning and using words and phrases that stop conflict in its tracks.

I remember a colleague of mine who was in the business world for his entire career. He loved to jibe me about being a teacher. Every time we got together, he would disparage the teaching profession. He knew I was a teacher and he loved to see my reaction. Of course, much to his pleasure, I reacted in passionate defense. Year after year, however, this became a tiresome tradition when we visited. Finally, one day, my colleague started in with his tirade about teaching and teachers in the profession, and I simply looked at him with a smile on my face and said, "You have an interesting perspective. I'll have to give that more thought." Then I changed the subject. Much to my amazement, his jaw dropped and he seemed to search for what to say next. It took the wind out of his sail and it was done so nicely.

Knowing phrases that stop conflict in its tracks is just one piece of the conflict-avoidance puzzle. The words we speak are actually less than 10% of our total communication. Body language and tone of voice are critical factors in how we communicate with other people. Body language communicates more than 80% of what we are trying to express. Tone of voice communicates more than 10% of what we are trying to convey.

So, if we have a comeback that should diffuse a conflict situation, such as "You have an interesting perspective. I'll have to give that some thought," the body language we use when we say those words and the tone of voice with which we speak them could render them either fighting words or words that diffuse a conflict situation. A calm and neutral tone of voice and relaxed body language will be the key factor as to whether the words actually stop conflict in its tracks.

Stopping Conflict in Its Tracks

When you find yourself caught in a verbal exchange that does not 'feel' right, then you may be dealing with bullying — intimidation, bulldozing, sarcasm, etc.

You may, also, simply be dealing with someone who is upset over a misunderstanding and unable to communicate clearly in the moment.

First: RECOGNIZE & PAY ATTENTION to your body signals — don't ignore the discomfort, adrenaline rush, etc.

Second: STOP, BREATHE, and THINK: "I CAN handle this!" (Positive self-talk)

Third: CONSCIOUSLY act! (As opposed to reacting.)

Be conscious of your body language and the words you choose:
Keep Your Power

Comebacks that don't escalate the conflict	Ask a question- S/he who asks the question has the power.
<ul><li>I see.</li><li>Thank you for letting me know how you feel.</li><li>Perhaps you are right.</li><li>I hear you.</li><li>Ouch! (Cues the other person that they are being hurtful. Sometimes they don't realize.)</li><li>I can see this upsets you.</li><li>I'm sorry you were hurt. That was not my intent.</li><li>I shouldn't have to defend myself, and I won't.</li><li>Excuse me, I'm not finished. (Say softly)</li><li>Agree with some of the statement but not all. (e.g. "You have a chip on your shoulder because you are short." Agree. Say, "Yes, I am short.")</li><li>You have an interesting perspective.</li><li>I'll have to give that some thought.</li><li>I will talk to you when you are calm. (Call "Time" & leave)</li><li>I will talk to you when I am calm. (Call "Time" & leave)</li></ul>	<ul><li>Why does that bother you?</li><li>How so?</li><li>Why do you ask?</li><li>What makes you say that?</li><li>I know you wouldn't have said that unless you had a good reason. Could you tell me what it was?</li></ul>

TIPS FOR SUCCESS

Be careful about tone of voice and/or lower your voice.
Avoid "should," "ought," and "you" statements.
Watch your body language. Respect personal space.

Tools for Collaborative Relationships

Communication: "What's Working?" Card

Good communication with coworkers and students is critical to successful inclusion. Often, our fears, agendas, and even enthusiasm get in the way of doing the kind of listening we need to do to foster good communication. Without effective communication, we make many assumptions about the people with whom we interact. Those assumptions might be very inaccurate and create tremendous conflict. Try to keep an open mind. Express how you feel and listen to other viewpoints. Good communication is necessary for the success of an inclusive classroom.

```
It's Working!

Not Working ☹

Let's Try ....
```

This card is a simple way to give feedback to your co-workers or individual members of the teaching team. I found it to be useful for reinforcing the positives. It can be delivered in person, or placed in a teacher mailbox. Simple 3X5 index cards work well.

Tips for Successful Collaboration

- Be flexible
- Look for success, not only in academic areas
- Make time to plan – even if it's just 10 minutes!
- Discuss problems only with each other
- Avoid using red ink to write notes to your colleagues

Pick-Me-Ups, Pick-U-Ups

- Compliment your colleagues where all can see
- Send a letter of appreciation and CC: the principal
- Remember special days with cards

Part 3: Positive Behavior Management

Be a Positive Role Model

Role-modeling appropriate behavior is a vital and necessary component of the effective approach to behavior management.

Beliefs and Attitudes of the Role Model

Who we are, what we think, and what we believe is revealed through our words and behavior. If we buy into the adage "Boys will be boys," our words and behavior will reflect it. If we have prejudices, they will be apparent. Everything we say and do provides the foundation for children's belief systems and attitudes. Sometimes, we are not even conscious of what we believe. Often, until we find ourselves reacting to a situation we feel strongly about, we do not really know that we have bought into a stereotype, a prejudice, or an attitude that limits us. Only when we become self-aware can we change our attitudes and beliefs to reflect the image we want our youth to model. Young people are more likely to do what we *do*, rather than what we say.

The Role Model and Discipline

Sometimes as teachers, parents, or adults in authority, we do not realize how we speak to children. Our tone of voice and choice of words, especially when disciplining, may be reinforcing negative patterns of behavior with children. This became glaringly obvious to me in my early years as a parent as I listened to my seven-year-old when she was angry with me. I often heard my words, my tone, and saw my facial expressions coming from her little body.

A small child does not categorize behavior. He does not say, "Oh, this is the tone I can use when I am an adult reprimanding my child." Rather, the behavior is interpreted as, "This is the tone I use when I am angry."

Traditionally, authoritarian discipline is used in schools and homes to manage children's behavior. An authoritarian approach, where directives and punishments are determined by the adult without enlisting the child in the formation of rules and consequences, produces youth who obey when in the presence of that particular adult. The downside to authoritarian discipline is that youth do not learn to self-discipline. They also learn to get what they want by using directives and meting out "punishments."

I do not advocate permissiveness; rather, I recommend an authoritative approach to discipline. An authoritative model involves students in the rule-making process. Consequences are established and firm limits on behavior are kept. An adult who uses an authoritative model of discipline is teaching students skills that are critical to sound character and conflict management.

When youth are involved in developing rules and consequences, they learn to use words to solve problems, to govern themselves, and to feel empowered. When rules deemed necessary by the adult are explained and consequences are logical, youth learn to be fair and trusting. When students who break the rules are involved in determining ways to "solve their own problem," they learn to control their own behavior. When young people are taught to see situations from another child's point of view and are required to make restitution to the hurt party, they learn empathy, forgiveness, and caring.

Treat Youth with Respect

Lack of respect from our youth is a common complaint heard from adults today. I am often astounded, however, by the lack of respect some adults show towards young people. Youth are often treated as lesser beings. Children are ordered around without a "please" or a "thank you." Because they are defenseless, they are often the scapegoats of misplaced anger. Their needs are often disregarded. I have witnessed adults ridicule youth for their failures and poke fun at their shortcomings.

All of us may be guilty of disrespecting our children's rights sometimes when we are tired, frustrated, or angry. It must be the exception, not the rule. When we do treat young people in a disrespectful way, the most empowering thing we can do for our children, and for ourselves, is to admit we made a mistake. When we admit our errors to young people, we teach them that it is okay to make mistakes. Mistakes are for learning. We are modeling a willingness to be honest, to own our behavior, and to learn from it. This is a powerful example to set for our youth. We want the same behavior from them when they make a mistake. Should we expect less of ourselves?

Discipline vs. Punishment: What is the Difference?[2]

PUNISHMENT

DISCIPLINE

- Punishment is <u>unexpected</u>. It is usually based on personal authority and arbitrary power.

- Discipline is <u>expected</u>. It is based on logical or natural consequences.

- Punishment is too severe.

- Discipline is fair and reasonable.

- Punishment reinforces failure. The individual has no options.

- Discipline reinforces success. Options are kept open as the individual is willing to take some responsibility.

- Punishment focuses on guilt, shame, blame, and fault.

- Discipline focuses on restitution and learning a better way.

- Punishment is meted out in the spirit of anger.

- Discipline is nurturing and caring.

---

[2] Based on work done by Diane Gossen, Perry Good, Barnes Boffey, and William Glasser.

RESPECT!

1. Listen carefully when students speak. Remain open-minded and objective. Consider their messages carefully. Avoid interrupting a student or offering unsolicited advice or criticism.

2. Respect students' personal space. Students may feel threatened and become agitated if you violate their personal space.

3. Use friendly gestures, not aggressive ones. Avoid "finger-pointing." Open, upturned palms may be more appropriate and effective.

4. Use preferred name. Ask each student how they would like to be addressed in the classroom. Only in rare instances would their chosen name be inappropriate.

5. Get on their level. Try to adopt their physical level. If they are seated, try kneeling or bending over, rather than standing over them.

6. Ask questions rather than make accusations. This assumes that the student is a responsible person. "Are you ready to begin?" rather than "Put your magazine away. It's time to start class." Use a concerned and kind tone.

7. Address problem behaviors privately. Reprimanding students in front of their peers may embarrass them unnecessarily. Speaking to them privately helps preserve their integrity and self-esteem.

Special Considerations for the Paraprofessional

Working within the Paraprofessional's Jurisdiction

Paraprofessionals usually face an additional challenge in the classroom, cafeteria, and playground: they have limited authority. Paraprofessionals usually cannot impact student grades. They rarely can keep students after school or schedule time in the day to work out a behavior contract with a student. They are usually dependent on another adult or authority to carry out the discipline for the offense that happened in their care.

Unfortunately, these realities make it difficult for the paraprofessional to develop rapport as an authority figure with students. Consequently, the paraprofessional must choose disciplinary methods that are primarily collaborative and least likely to set the stage for a power struggle. This also allows the paraprofessional to develop a positive rapport with students.

Also, paraprofessionals should not be asked to contact parents about discipline problems that have occurred during the day. These should be discussed with the teacher or school administrator.

Violent Students: Proceed with Caution

Special training is required to properly diffuse situations involving students with a tendency toward violent outbursts. Physically violent students and students with serious emotional disturbance may need wrap-around[3] services. Paraprofessionals and teachers working with physically violent students need intensive specialized training to respond effectively to violent behaviors.

---

[3] A wrap-around support system is a collaborative effort involving agencies and schools to provide coordinated services to a student and/or a student's family.

General Behavior Management Tips

Behaviors to Avoid When Disciplining

- Shouting loudly or continually
- Nagging
- Pushing or pulling students about
- Confronting in an accusatory tone
- Engaging in banter/arguing
- Sarcasm
- Threatening (as opposed to presenting logical consequences or choices)
- Jumping to conclusions
- Assuming that students who are regularly in trouble are always to blame for incidents
- Losing your temper

Techniques That Build Rapport & Foster Better Behavior

- Treating students with respect
- Treating students in a firm, friendly, and quiet way
- Giving plenty of praise/rewards for appropriate behavior
- Making a note of all serious incidents that need follow-up
- Knowing where there is help in case of an emergency
- Dealing with matters consistently as set out in staff procedure or as agreed upon by responsible staff
- Keep a notebook to record good and poor behavior; this allows you to follow up on all incidents
- Attempt to reprimand students quietly and privately

If you have to discipline someone, make a determined effort to repair the relationship once the discipline is over.

Choice: Encourage Choice and Decision-Making

Offering students choices is the first line of defense for avoiding behavior problems. Additionally, five specific areas can be enhanced when individuals are allowed to make choices and decisions for themselves.

Choice:
1. May reduce or prevent problem behaviors.
2. Can offer independence.
3. Can increase motivation and productivity.
4. Can prevent learned helplessness.
5. Can increase attention to task.

Scripts for Offering Choice

- You can do any 10 questions/problems on page 103.
- Do the 'X' assignments in any order you choose.
- Choose 3 of 10 activities.
- Choose where to sit for independent activities.
- You may have a one-minute break now or a three-minute break in 10 minutes.
- When a student balks at an assignment, such as, "Write the spelling words three times each," you might respond, "Come up with a better plan to learn the material and present it to me."

Offering Choice-Making Opportunities[4]

Type of Choice	Situation	Question Format
BETWEEN ACTIVITIES: Provide a choice between two or more activities during a routine	**LIBRARY:** Listen to a book on tape or ask the librarian to read a book out loud	**CLOSED:** Would you like to do your spelling or science? **OPEN:** Which subject would you like?
WITHIN ACTIVITIES/ MATERIALS: Provide a choice between two or more items within a specific task	**SNACK:** Apple or grapes **SPELLING:** Quiz a friend or write words out on a worksheet	**CLOSED:** Would you like an apple or grapes? **OPEN:** What type of fruit would you like?
REFUSAL: Before beginning a task, provide a choice of whether or not to participate	**ACADEMICS:** Do you want to complete the activity so that you have time to take part in the review game, or do you want to spend all of your time sitting out the activity alone?	**CLOSED:** Give two definite choices **OPEN:** Let student present options
WHO: At the beginning of a task, provide a choice of whom to work or play with	**LUNCH:** Would you like to sit with your friends or the teacher at lunch?	**CLOSED:** Same **OPEN:** With whom would you like to work?
WHERE: At the beginning of a task, provide a choice of where to do the activity	**ACADEMICS:** Would you like to sit at your desk or the study carrel to work?	**CLOSED:** Same **OPEN:** Where would you like to complete your reading assignment?
WHEN: Provide a choice of when to participate in an activity	**ACADEMICS:** Would you like to do your reading now or after gym?	**CLOSED:** Same **OPEN:** When would you like to go to the park?
TERMINATE ACTIVITY: Periodically during the task, provide the choice to quit	**INDIVIDUAL WORK TIME:** Let me know when you need to stop and take a break	**CLOSED:** Do you want to stop or continue? **OPEN:** Let me know when you are done.

---

[4] Adapted from Bambara, L. M., & Koger, F. (1996). Self-scheduling as a choice-making strategy. In D. Browder (Ed.), Innovations: Opportunities for daily choice making (pp. 33-41). Washington, DC: American Association on Mental Retardation.

Possible Scripts for Responding to Student Behavior

Sometimes, it helps to have an idea of how to respond to student behavior in a way that encourages students to own their actions, does not create a power struggle, and is consistent and effective. Scripts should be stated in a calm tone of voice, with normal voice volume. Be careful not to get into the student's space; rather, convey non-threatening yet self-assured body language. Following are some suggestions for response.

For disruption or arguing
"Eric, that's disrupting. Yelling out 'A bunch of idiots are sitting on the porch!' could be offensive to some. Is there another way you can say that same thing in a way that may not be seen as offensive?"

"Eric, that's arguing. What do you need to do if you think someone is 'getting into it with you'? You need to make a good choice here."

"Eric, that's arguing. You need to immediately stop in [five to ten seconds] or you will be ... [state consequence]."

For refusing to work or participate appropriately
Say, "Eric, that's refusal. Might _____ be a better choice?"

If Eric responds positively, 'notice' the positive choice (reinforce).

If behavior continues...

Say, "Eric, that's continued refusal. What is it you were asked to do? Please make a good choice for yourself so the **adults** don't have to make it for you."

If Eric responds positively, 'notice' the positive choice (reinforce).

If behavior continues...

Say, "Eric, that's continued refusal. You need to do what you were asked to do, or... [state the consequence]."

For tardiness to class

Say, "Eric, it is X minutes past the time you needed to be in class. That is tardiness. Next time you are tardy … [state the consequence]."

Say, "Eric, it is X minutes past the time you needed to be in class. That is tardiness. The consequence for tardiness is … [state the consequence]."

Possible consequences:
- Owe minutes right after school.
- Owe minutes before school – arrange with parents to bring him in early.
  - ❖ Use detention time to build rapport and teach, not preach, about good choices and how they might help him be more successful at getting what he wants.
- Lose pass privileges if he was on a pass.

For having difficulty settling down
- "You can _____ as soon as you get quiet. This offer is good for 10 seconds."
- "You can sit anywhere you like, as long as you don't block the door or interfere with anyone else's learning."
- "You can _____ as soon as you finish _____ section of your work."

For bullying
- "Language please!"
- "We don't say that here!"
- "Embarrassing someone isn't a joke!"
- "That is hate language and it's against the law."

When the student attacks the adult to try to turn the tables
Student: "You smell!"
Adult, in a matter-of-fact, firm tone of voice: "What's important in this conversation is you (or what happened)." Then continue to address the student's behavior.

When students try to debate (Don't take the bait!)
Adult: "Johnny, sit down."
Student: "Why do I have to sit down? Jane isn't sitting down!"
Adult: "Johnny, sit down."
Student: "Why? You are always picking on me!"
Adult: "Johnny, sit down."
Repeat in a calm, firm monotone until Johnny gets tired of hearing the 'broken record' and sits down.

Behavioral Support Strategies for the Playground and Cafeteria

STRATEGY	EXPLANATION
State the expectation	Tell the student what to do and how you want them to do it.
Proximity	▪ Stand closer to the student's shoulder or arm while maintaining focus on the issue at hand. ▪ Lay your palm on the table or desk by the student's arm while maintaining focus on the student's behavior.
Gentle touch	Touch the student's shoulder or arm while maintaining focus on the issue. *Use ONLY if you feel this will de-escalate any conflict between you and the student.
Nonverbal cues	Smile, nod, or give a thumbs-up to reinforce appropriate behaviors.
Direct verbal cues	In a quiet and private manner, tell the student exactly how you want him or her to behave. End the statement by saying "Thank you." Step away from the student. During the interaction, act calm and dispassionate, regardless of how you actually feel.
Offer a choice	Offer the student a choice in which the options are incompatible with continuing the behavior. For example, when a student refuses to stop pushing or cutting in line, you could ask, "Do you want to stay where you are in line, or do you want to go to the end of the line? Make a good choice for yourself."

Playground Strategies

- Have different parts of the playground set out for games, quiet activities, playing with balls, etc. Often conflict is triggered because children run into each other while playing, or children are excluded.

- Be vigilant watching over the students. The more staff that are actively supervising or engaging groups of students in games, the less likelihood of problems occurring.

- Deal with bullying and intimidation immediately. (Telling children to "Go and work it out" makes the victim feel invalidated, resentful, and powerless, and allows the bullying child to believe you do not care enough about it to take the time to deal with it. Some students bully simply because they can get away with it.)

- If you have a real and persistent problem with poor behavior on the playground, keep a camera handy and take pictures. Often, just pointing the camera at the problem area will immediately stop problems. Students do not want a picture proving they were the cause of the problem.

Behavior Management for 1-1 & Small Groups

Using non-confrontational strategies for managing minor discipline problems or the early stages of potential problems can significantly reduce problems in the classroom. Depending on the strategies chosen, behavior may de-escalate or escalate. The goal of this section is to suggest strategies that de-escalate conflict or potential behavior problems.

Cueing Students to Redirect or Reinforce

Often the best approach to managing student behavior is to quietly cue the student to stop their inappropriate behavior, return to task, or to continue positive behavior. Often simply making eye contact with a student and giving him or her a certain look or gesture is all that is needed to communicate your message. Avoid doing things that may embarrass students.

Ways to cue students:
- Make eye contact.

- Use physical gestures (i.e., raising your hand in silence or enlisting a pre-taught signal known to the student).

- Tap or snap your fingers, cough or clear your throat to get the student's attention and redirect.

- Facial expressions (i.e., smile).

- Body language (Be careful to be non-threatening. Avoid getting into the student's space).

- Create a simple stop/go cue card. One side is red and the other green. When you want a behavior to stop, show the red side. When you want a behavior to continue, show the green side. Use green to affirm or reinforce positive behavior.

- Create a pictorial behavior management cue card. This is especially helpful with students in the autistic spectrum.

Behavior Management Cue Card

1. Create your cue card to match redirection and praise you frequently state in class.
2. Stick the cue card on the top corner of each student's desk. (Laminate it, use shipping tape, etc. to make it sturdy.)
3. Rather than disturb the class with a verbal correction or embarrass a student with verbal praise, walk up to the student's desk and:
   a. Make eye contact.
   b. Point to the picture on the card that represents what you want to say.
   c. Walk away. (Do not say anything or engage in banter.)

Optional: You might also punch a hole in the laminated card and put it on a lanyard or keep it in your pocket. This is especially helpful if you cannot tape them to the desk.

Strategic Ignoring

Sometimes the best way to deal with student misbehavior is to ignore it.

When might it be best to ignore behavior?
- When the inappropriate behavior is unintentional or not likely to reoccur.

- When the student's goal is to get attention through misbehaving.

- When ignoring it will decrease misbehavior by not reinforcing it.

- When it is out of your area of jurisdiction.

When is it best not to ignore behavior?
- When there is physical danger or harm to yourself, others, or the student.

- When a student disrupts the classroom through inappropriate behavior.

- When a student violates class or school rules.

- When the behavior interferes with the student's or other students' learning.

- When the inappropriate behavior will incite other students to join in.

- When other students reinforce the misbehavior by snickering, laughing, and otherwise giving positive – or even negative – feedback.

Proximity Control

Stand or sit near a student who is experiencing difficulty. Also, circulating around the classroom will often help keep students on task because of your proximity to them. Students know you are aware of their behavior and will usually stop any inappropriate behavior quickly. This allows the classroom teacher to continue teaching without interrupting the lesson or the flow of the activity. As a caution, it's important not to reinforce negative behavior by calling attention to the student.

Communication could be the Solution!

Sometimes students become frustrated and violent because they are unable to verbally express what they need or want. Also, transitions are often difficult for students with special needs. It may be helpful to use pictures or photos as a communication tool. Pictures can be downloaded from the internet from clipart sources or Google Images. There are also software programs like Mayer-Johnson's Boardmaker® specifically designed for this purpose.

- Put VELCRO® on the backs of the photos.
- Put the other half of the VELCRO on a piece of tag board or even an open file folder.
- Arrange the pictures in the order of the student's daily schedule. Depending on the mental age or disability level of the student, you may need to help him or her with this at first. Say, "Now it's time for music," and hand-over-hand help him remove the picture of music and put it in a designated place (maybe an envelope that's attached to the board).

Also, have photos/pictures for the student to use to communicate his or her wishes and needs with you, such as drink, snack, bathroom, etc. In this way the student can use the pictures to show you what he wants.

It might also be helpful to learn a few American Sign Language signs, such as stop, no, yes, bathroom, walk, etc., and then use them to reinforce your verbal cues.

Problem Solving Mind Map
Use the problem solving mind map to help students work through tough choices. The key when working through the process is for the adult to be non-judgmental.

Problem Solving Mind Map

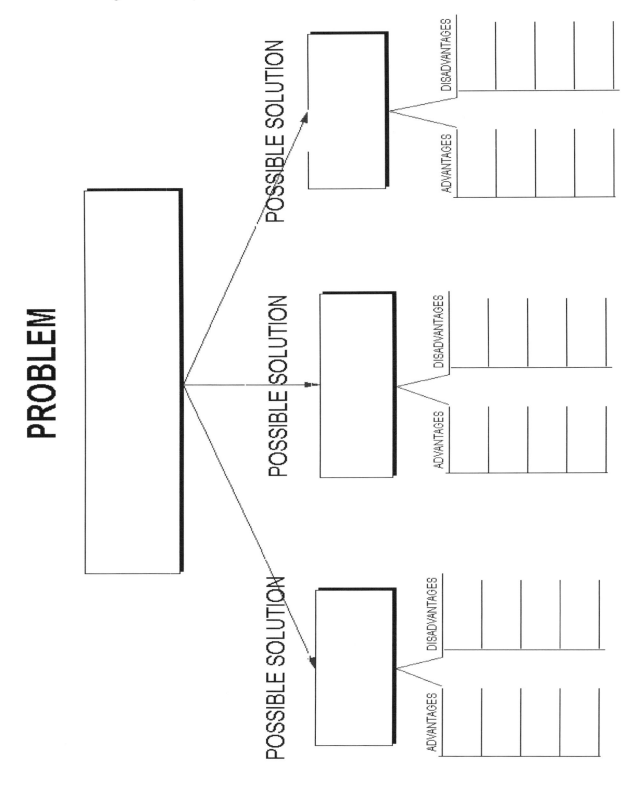

Tips & Tools to Focus and Calm Students

For Students Having Difficulty with Attention and Distractibility

- Assign students Task Buddies to help keep partner on task.

- Seat students near the center of instruction.

- Seat distractible students surrounded by well-focused students.

- Allow quiet fidget things, doodling, or mandalas to help students focus. Trade student's noisy thing with a teacher-approved fidget thing.

- Provide study carrels or partitions to reduce visual distractions during seatwork or test-taking as appropriate. (This should be a student choice, not a punishment.)

- Provide sound-reducing headsets for students to minimize auditory distractions.

- During silent reading, consider allowing students to sit on the floor if they ask. Some students become amazingly focused when they carve out their own space on the floor or in a corner of the classroom.

- Allow students to ask buddies for clarification on seatwork.

- Consider allowing ADHD students to "tutor" other students in areas of strength. This often brings out focused, caring behavior and encourages self-esteem.

- Silence the pen tapper with the sponge from a curler.

- Give an angry or over-excited student some Silly Putty® or TackyTac to knead as a calming strategy.

- Provide inexpensive craft rings threaded with beads to fidgeting students for calming.

- Stick a soft, fuzzy side of a strip of sticky-backed VELCRO to the underside of a desk for students who "pick" at things. Agree on a non-verbal cue to encourage the student to "pick" at the VELCRO strip instead of other less desirable places.

Brain Gym®: A Wakeup Call to the Brain[5]

Brain Gym® is a series of exercises that enables the brain to work at its best. The techniques are a composite of many differing sciences based predominantly upon neurobiology. It has been found to facilitate learning in learning-disabled students. However, the results of using Brain Gym have proven to be highly effective for all learners. There is even evidence that Brain Gym can be used for psychological disorders as well.

Teachers will find these exercises enhance student performance before test-taking in particular, but they also work before listening to lectures and studying. They also may relieve stress.

How does Brain Gym work? Carla Hannaford, Ph.D., neurophysiologist, states in "Smart Moves" that our bodies are very much a part of all our learning, and that learning is not an isolated "brain" function. Every nerve and cell is a network contributing to our intelligence and our learning capability. She states, "Movement activates the neural wiring throughout the body, making the whole body the instrument of learning." Hannaford states that "sensation" forms the basis of concepts from which "thinking" evolves.

Brain Gym exercises consider our bi-cameral brain. The brain has a left and a right hemisphere, each one doing certain distinct tasks. Often one side of our brain works more than the other, depending upon the tasks we are doing or how we have developed as human beings. If the two brains are working fully and sharing information across the corpus callosum, there is a balance of brain function. Without this balance, there is always going to be something that is not understood or remembered. Brain Gym assists in integrating the two brains, which gives us full capacity for problem solving or learning.

We are also "electrical" beings and our brains' neurons work by electrical connections. Drinking water has been found to be the best thing we can do to facilitate the thinking process because of its capacity to conduct electricity and assist cell function. As Carla Hannaford says, "Water comprises more of the brain (with estimates of 90%) than of any other organ of the body." Thus, a

---

[5] Adapted from an article by Ruth Trimble (trimble@hawaii.edu)
Much of the factual material for this article is taken from "Smart Moves" by Carla Hannaford, Ph.D. and Dr. Paul Dennison and his EduK® literature. Please cite these authors when using this material. Permission to use my data is given, but it constitutes only my opinion and limited practical experience and is not in any way intended to represent the official Brain Gym or EduK view, nor give permission to reproduce the detailed exercises designed by the other authors without citing them.

simple drink of water before a test or before going to class can have a profound effect on our brains' readiness to work. Unfortunately, coffee or soda will have the opposite effect since these will upset the electrolytes in the brain. The exercises that you see here are designed to make us a whole-brain learner. Some simple but effective ways to wake up the brain and get it working instantly and optimally are listed on the following pages.

Before any of the following exercises, DRINK a glass of water.

"HOOK-UPS"

This works well for nerves before a test or special event such as making a speech. Any time there is nervousness or anxiety, this will bring a sense of calm.

1. Sit for this activity and cross the right leg over the left at the ankles.
2. Take your right wrist and cross it over the left wrist and link up the fingers so that the right wrist is on top.
3. Now bend the elbows out and gently turn the fingers in towards the body until they rest on the sternum (breastbone) in the center of the chest.
4. Stay in this position.
5. Keep the ankles crossed and the wrists crossed and then breathe evenly in this position for a few minutes.
6. You will be noticeably calmer after that time.

Ruth Trimble states, "My student test scores have gone up because of Brain Gym. I have students achieving far higher scores than I have seen using the same screening and testing methods for the past six years. The ones who are doing Brain Gym are accomplishing so much more."

Mandalas: Focus, Calm, and Creative Inspiration

- Working from the center to the edge: Broadens attention

- Working from the edge to center: Focuses attention

- Relaxes the body

- Activates the right brain

- Visual prompt/structural map for writing feelings in a poem, song, or composition

- "Tilt the brain so language comes out differently" –Caryn Mirriam-Goldberg, author of "Write Where you Are" from Free Spirit Press

A source for mandalas can be found at http://www.mandali.com/

Color Your Own Mandala

Sample from Monique Mandali, *Everyone's Mandala Coloring Book*,
http://www.mandali.com/

Dealing with Tattling

The "It's not fair!" comment tends to peak amongst fourth graders. Children seem to notice every other child's infractions. Tattling is still common. Some children refuse to tattle because of social pressure, but they may "get even" instead. Help them become aware of their anger over an injustice. Teach them to stop and think before they react. What are the alternatives to tattling or retaliation?

Validate students' feelings. When a child tattles, often all they need is validation of their feelings. A question such as "How did that feel when Janie called you that name?" lets the child feel heard. To follow up with empathy regarding their feelings and options for what they can do next usually leaves students feeling like they have been heard and they now have tools to handle the situation.

Teachers and parents often discourage tattling. By fifth grade, tattling is a major social taboo. The relief that upper elementary teachers and parents have from tattling holds hidden dangers. I asked a fifth grade class if they would tell if they knew someone had a gun in their backpack. To my astonishment, half of the class said they would not tell. They explained that it would be tattling. It is social suicide to tattle. In addition, telling might put them in danger. I realized students needed to be taught that telling an authority when someone has a weapon, or someone is physically threatened, is following a safety rule. Kids are familiar with safety rules regarding fire, going with strangers, and riding bicycles. They have a certain amount of respect for these rules. They are accepted. Personal safety needs to be addressed in the same way. When we use authority to insure personal safety, it is not tattling, it is following a safety rule. The consequences of *not* telling must be made clear to the students.

The Difference between Tattling and Telling

A TATTLE IS WHEN SOMEONE:

- Is trying to get attention for him or herself.
- Is trying to get someone else in trouble.
- Is trying to get his or her way.
- Can handle the problem by himself or herself.

A TELLING IS WHEN SOMEONE:

- Is trying to get help for a psychologically or physically harmful or dangerous situation.
- Is trying to get help for a scary occurrence or if someone needs protection.
- Needs help from an adult to solve the problem.
- Is trying to keep people safe.

Part 4: Academic Support

This section includes strategies for one-to-one & small group instruction. These strategies can also be used with whole class instruction by paraprofessionals, as well as general and special education teachers.

Recent scientific research has confirmed that we all have different learning preferences and that we all learn best with strategies and techniques that honor our learning preferences. Brain research has taught us that we all, regardless of learning style, process information in ways specific to our unique abilities. This section provides the reader with simple, proven tools to help students increase academic performance and make their learning experience more rewarding and productive. Tools provided will help students succeed at any grade level.

Understanding Special Needs

What is Exceptionality under Federal Law?[6]

Assessment and Federal Law

The Individuals with Disabilities Education Act (IDEA), Public Law 101-476, lists 13 separate categories of disabilities under which students may be eligible for special education and related services.

These categories are:

Autism: classified as a neurodevelopmental disorder that manifests in delays of "social interaction, language as used in social communication, or symbolic or imaginative play," with "onset prior to age 3 years," according to the Diagnostic and Statistical Manual of Mental Disorders.

Deafness: a hearing impairment so severe that the student is impaired in processing linguistic information, with or without amplification.

Deaf-blindness: simultaneous hearing and visual impairments.

Hearing Impairment: a defect in the ability to perceive sound, whether permanent or fluctuating.

Mental Retardation: significantly subaverage general intellectual functioning, existing concurrently with deficits in adaptive behavior.

- **EMH – "Educable mentally handicapped."** An eligibility category under IDEA including students whose cognitive development is approximately one-half to three-fourths the average rate and is accompanied by similar delays in adaptive behavior.
- **MH – "Trainable mentally handicapped."** An eligibility category under IDEA including students whose cognitive development is approximately one-fourth to one-half the average rate and is accompanied by similar delays in adaptive behavior.

Multiple Disabilities: the manifestation of two or more disabilities (such as mental retardation-blindness), the combination of which requires special accommodation for maximal learning.

---

[6] Waterman, B (2000, April 20). Assessing Children for the Presence of a Disability. Retrieved November 3, 2006, from Kidsource Web site: http://www.kidsource.com/NICHCY/assessing.1.html

---

Orthopedic Impairment: physical disabilities, including congenital impairments, impairments caused by disease, and impairments from other causes.

Other Health Impairment: limited strength, vitality, or alertness due to chronic or acute health problems.

Serious Emotional Disturbance: a disability where a student of typical intelligence has difficulty, over time and to a marked degree, building satisfactory interpersonal relationships; responds inappropriately either behaviorally or emotionally under normal circumstances; demonstrates a pervasive mood of unhappiness; or has a tendency to develop physical symptoms or fears.

Specific Learning Disability: a disorder in one or more of the basic psychological processes involved in understanding or in using language, spoken or written, which may manifest itself in an imperfect ability to listen, think, speak, read, write, spell, or do mathematical calculations.

Speech or Language Impairment: a communication disorder such as stuttering, impaired articulation, a language impairment, or a voice impairment.

Traumatic Brain Injury: an acquired injury to the brain caused by an external physical force, resulting in total or partial functional disability, a psychosocial impairment, or both.

Visual Impairment: a visual difficulty (including blindness) that, even with correction, adversely affects a student's educational performance.

What is a Specific Learning Disability?

Generally speaking, students may be diagnosed with learning disabilities if they are of average or above-average intelligence and there is a significant discrepancy between their academic achievement and their intellectual ability. The diagnosis of a learning disability is usually made by a psychologist trained in administering and interpreting psychoeducational assessments.

Psychoeducational assessments typically include, but are not limited to, an assessment of intellectual functioning and a battery of achievement tests. Psychologists use the results of these assessments to understand how individuals receive, process, retain, and communicate information. Since the act of information processing cannot be observed, it is often difficult to diagnose specific learning disabilities, determine their impact, and recommend appropriate accommodations. Learning disabilities usually fall within four broad categories:

- **Spoken language**: listening and speaking
- **Written language**: reading, writing, and spelling
- **Arithmetic**: calculation and concepts
- **Reasoning**: organization and integration of ideas and thoughts

A person with a learning disability may have discrepancies in one or all of these categories. Learning disabilities may also be present along with other disabilities such as mobility and sensory impairments, brain injuries, Attention Deficit Disorder/Attention Deficit Hyperactivity Disorder (ADD/ADHD), and psychiatric disabilities.

Functional Limitations

"A specific learning disability is unique to the individual and can be manifested in a variety of ways. Therefore, accommodations for a student with a specific learning disability must be tailored to the individual. Deficiencies in the ability to process information make learning and/or expressing ideas difficult for a person with a learning disability. Described below are some of the functional limitations that may require accommodation. A student with a learning disability may have one or more of these limitations."[7]

- **Auditory processing**: The student may have difficulty processing information communicated through lectures or class discussions.
- **Visual processing**: The student may have difficulty processing information communicated via overhead projection, through video, in graphs and charts, by email, or within web-based distance learning courses.
- **Information processing speed**: The student may process information more slowly than the average person.
- **Reading, decoding, and comprehending skills**: The student may be a slow reader due to a need for additional time to decode and comprehend written material.

---

[7] Burgstahler, Sheryl (2004). Academic Accommodations for Students with Learning Disabilities. Retrieved November 3, 2006, from University of Washington Web site: http://www.washington.edu/doit/Brochures/Academics/accomm_ld.html

- **Abstract and general reasoning**: The student may have difficulty understanding the context of subjects such as philosophy and logic which require high-level reasoning skills.

- **Memory (long-term, short-term, visual, auditory)**: The student may have difficulty with the storing and/or recalling of information during short or long time periods or presented visually or auditorily.

- **Spoken and written language skills**: The student may have difficulty with spelling, (e.g., mixing up letters) or with speaking (e.g., reversing words or phrases).

- **Mathematical calculation skills and word problems**: The student may have difficulty manipulating numbers, may sometimes invert numbers, and may have difficulty converting problems described in words to mathematical expressions.

- **Executive functioning (planning and time management)**: The student may have difficulty breaking larger projects into smaller sub-projects, creating and following a timeline, and meeting deadlines.

Related Terminology[8]

- **Chronologically age-appropriate**: A standard by which students' activities may be evaluated. Instruction and materials should be directed at the student's actual age, rather than to the interests and tastes of younger students.

- **Cognitive**: A term which refers to reasoning or intellectual capacity.

- **Disability**: A physical, sensory, cognitive, or affective impairment that causes the student to need special education. NOTE: There are significant differences in the definitions of disability in IDEA and Section 504.

- **Due process:** In general, due process includes the elements of notice, opportunity to be heard, and to defend ones' self. With regard to IDEA, due process refers to a specific set of procedures described in 23 IAC Part 226. With regard to Section 504, procedures are less clearly specified. With regard to student discipline matters, the amount of process that is due is largely dependent upon the degree of jeopardy involved.

---

[8] Rogers, J (2006). A Parent's Guide to Special Ed/Special Needs. Retrieved November 3, 2006, from The Council for Disability Rights Web site: http://www.disabilityrights.org/glossary.htm Not copyrighted.

- **Fine motor:** Functions that require tiny muscle movements. For example, writing or typing would require fine motor movement.

- **Functional curriculum:** A curriculum focused on practical life skills and usually taught in community-based settings with concrete materials that are a regular part of everyday life. The purpose of this type of instruction is to maximize the student's generalization to real life use of his/her skills.

- **Gross motor:** Functions which require large muscle movements. For example, walking or jumping would require gross motor movement.

- **Heterogeneous grouping:** An educational practice in which students of diverse abilities are placed within the same instructional groups. This practice is usually helpful in the integration of students with disabilities.

- **Homogeneous grouping:** An educational practice in which students of similar abilities are placed within the same instructional groups. This practice usually serves as a barrier to the integration of students with disabilities.

- **IEP - Individualized Education Plan:** The document developed at an IEP meeting which sets the standard by which subsequent special education services are usually determined appropriate.

- **IEP meeting:** A gathering required at least annually under IDEA in which an IEP is developed for a student receiving special education.

- **IDEA - Individuals with Disabilities Education Act:** Law that modifies and extends the Education for All Handicapped Students Act (EHA).

- **LRE:** Least restrictive environment. A requirement of IDEA.

- **Occupational therapy:** A special education-related service which is usually focused upon the development of a student's fine motor skills and/or the identification of adapted ways of accomplishing activities of daily living, when a student's disabilities preclude doing those tasks in typical ways (e.g. modifying clothing so a person without arms can dress himself/herself).

- **Permanent record:** A brief document upon which essential information is entered and preserved. The contents of the permanent record are specified in the Illinois Student Records Act.

- **Placement:** The setting in which the special education service is delivered to the student. It must be derived from the student's IEP.

- **Section 504:** Provision of the Rehabilitation Act of 1973 which prohibits recipients of federal funds from discrimination against persons with disabilities.

- **Supplementary aids and services:** Accommodations which could permit a student to profit from instruction in the least restrictive environment. They are required under IDEA.

- **Total communication:** An instructional strategy in which paraprofessionals or teachers instruct students with severe hearing loss both by speaking to them and by using sign language. The theory is that if the students can learn to speak, then the stimulation is being presented. Even if they do not learn to speak, they will still be provided with a language-rich environment.

- **Visual-motor:** Coordination of what is seen with an action. For example, one uses visual-motor coordination when catching a ball.

How the Brain Learns

How We Learn According to Brain Research

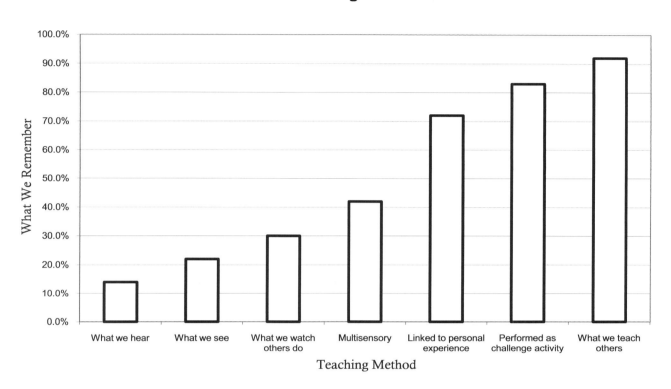

Sources:
Leonard, 1994
Glasser, 1996 Control Theory in the Classroom
Dryden, Gorden & Vos, Dr. Jeannette, 1994 The Learning Revolution: A Life-Long Learning Program for the World's Finest Computer Your Amazing Brain

Multiple Intelligence / Learning Style

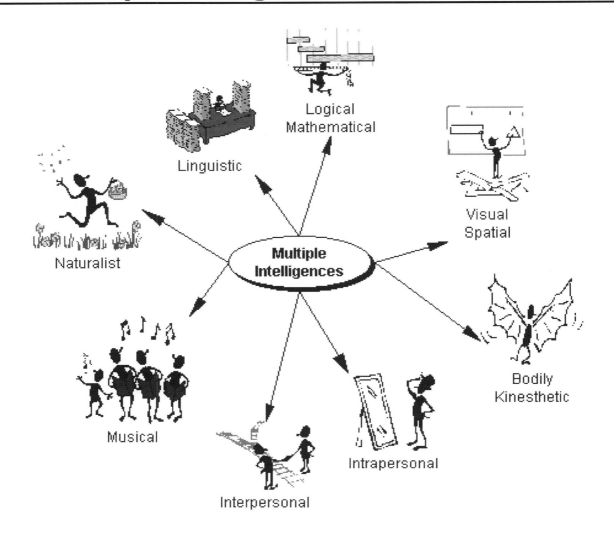

Assessment Checklist for Multiple Intelligence

Instructions:
Read through these checklists to determine your learning style. Put a checkmark near the bullets that describe how you learn best. The boxes that have the most checks may indicate the type of learner you might be. This is not a test. It is simply a tool to start thinking about how you might learn best. Use the strategy pages following this assessment for study suggestions to differentiate instruction. If it works for the student, keep doing it! If it doesn't work, try something else.

Use these checklists with your students so that they might determine their Multiple Intelligence Style.

Do you...	Do you...
☐ Tell tall tales, jokes, and stories ☐ Have a good memory ☐ Enjoy word games ☐ Enjoy reading and writing ☐ Have a good vocabulary for your age ☐ Have good verbal communication ☐ Enjoy crossword puzzles ☐ Appreciate nonsense rhymes, puns, tongue twisters, etc. ☐ Spell words accurately	☐ Ask questions about how things work ☐ Enjoy math activities ☐ Enjoy playing chess, checkers, or other strategy games ☐ Enjoy logic puzzles or brain teasers ☐ Use higher-order thinking skills ☐ Have an interest in patterns, categories, and relationships ☐ Like doing and creating experiments ☐ Do arithmetic problems in your head quickly ☐ Have a good sense of cause and effect
Are you a linguistic learner?	Are you a logical-mathematical learner?
Do you...	Do you...
☐ Excel in one or more sport or physical art ☐ Move, twitch, tap, or fidget when seated for a long time ☐ Enjoy taking things apart and putting them back together ☐ Feel the need to touch new objects ☐ Enjoy running, jumping, or wrestling ☐ Express yourself dramatically ☐ Still enjoy modeling clay and finger painting ☐ Like to work with your hands ☐ Like to mimic other people's gestures or mannerisms ☐ Tend to report different physical sensations while thinking or working	☐ Daydream more than your peers ☐ Enjoy art activities ☐ Like visual presentations ☐ Enjoy puzzles and mazes ☐ Understand more from pictures than words while reading ☐ Doodle on paper ☐ Still love construction sets: Legos, K'nex, Capsela, etc. ☐ Often invent things ☐ Draw things that others would find difficult to draw ☐ Read maps, charts, and diagrams more easily than text
Are you a bodily kinesthetic learner?	Are you a spatial learner?

Use these checklists with your students so that they might determine their Multiple Intelligence Style.

Do you...	Do you...
☐ Recognize off-key music ☐ Remember melodies ☐ Play a musical instrument or sing in a choir ☐ Speak or move rhythmically ☐ Tap rhythmically as you work ☐ Find that you are sensitive to environmental noise ☐ Respond favorably to music ☐ Sing songs that you learn outside of class ☐ Tend to be a discriminating listener ☐ Create your own songs and melodies Are you a musical learner?	☐ Enjoy socializing with peers ☐ Act as a natural leader ☐ Give advice to friends who have problems ☐ Feel you are street-smart ☐ Belong to clubs, committees, or other organizations ☐ Like to play group games like poker or monopoly ☐ Have one or more close friends ☐ Show concern for others ☐ Easily notice and perceive people's moods, intentions, and motivations ☐ Respond well to other people's feelings Are you an interpersonal learner?
Do you...	Do you...
☐ Have a sense of independence or a strong will ☐ Have a realistic sense of your strengths ☐ Have a good sense of self-direction ☐ Prefer working alone to working with others ☐ Learn from your failures and successes ☐ Feel you are insightful and self-aware ☐ Adapt well to your environment ☐ Feel you are well aware of your own emotions, strengths, and limitations ☐ Feel you are self-disciplined ☐ March to the beat of a different drummer in your style of living and learning Are you an intrapersonal learner?	☐ Enjoy labeling and identifying nature ☐ Find you are sensitive to changes in weather ☐ Easily distinguish differences among cars, sneakers, and jewelry, etc. Are you a naturalist learner?

Suggestions for Learning according to Multiple Intelligence

For Verbal/Linguistic Learners	For Logical Mathematical Learners
☐ Allow options for students to choose from when assigning projects, research, study, and practice ☐ Create radio or TV advertisements (see History Project below) ☐ Debate current events ☐ Create crossword puzzles ☐ Teach the class the steps to... ☐ Write a script	☐ Compare and contrast ideas ☐ Create a timeline ☐ Classify concepts/objects/materials ☐ Read or design maps ☐ Create a computer program ☐ Create story problems for... ☐ Design and conduct an experiment on... ☐ Use a Venn diagram to explain... ☐ Teach using technology
For Body Kinesthetic Learners	**For Visual Spatial Learners**
☐ Create hands-on projects ☐ Conduct hands-on experiments ☐ Create human sculptures to illustrate situations ☐ Design something that requires applying math concepts ☐ Re-enact great moments from history ☐ Study body language from different cultural situations ☐ Make task or puzzle cards for ...	☐ Make visual organizer or memory model of the material being learned (give copies to other students in the class) ☐ Graph the results of a survey or results from a course of study ☐ Create posters or flyers ☐ Create collages ☐ Draw maps ☐ Study the art of a culture ☐ Color-code the process of...
For Musical Rhythmic Learners	**For Interpersonal Learners**
☐ Create "raps" (key dates, math, poems) ☐ Identify social issues through lyrics ☐ Analyze different historical periods through their music ☐ Make up sounds for different math operations or processes ☐ Use music to enhance the learning of... ☐ Write a new ending to a song so that it explains...	☐ Analyze a story ☐ Review material/concepts/books orally ☐ Discuss/debate controversial issues ☐ Find relationships between objects, cultures, situations ☐ Role-play a conversation with an important historical figure ☐ Solve complex word problems in a group ☐ Peer tutor the subject being learned
For Intrapersonal Learners	**For Naturalist Learners**
☐ Keep a journal to demonstrate learning ☐ Analyze historical personalities ☐ Imagine self as character in history, or scientist discovering a cure, or mathematician working a theory and describe or write about what you imagine to demonstrate learning	☐ Sort and classify content in relation to the natural world ☐ Interact with nature through field trips ☐ Encourage learning in natural surroundings ☐ Categorize facts about...

Setting up the Environment

Paraprofessionals do not always have control over the work environment. When it is possible to influence the learning environment the following considerations and strategies are recommended.

Provide a comfortable place to work without distractions.

Calm restless students with wordless music at 60 beats per minute or less.

- Helps with attention issues and sensory processing
- Supports organized body movement
- Assists active engagement of the learner
- Increases both alpha and beta brain waves which are associated with a quiet, alert state that is receptive for learning
- Helps to provide structure for organized thinking, e.g. writing reports or papers, activities that involve planning

Suggestions:

- Native American Flute
- Peruvian Mantra
- Mozart for Learning (Caution: Some classical is too rambunctious. The key is 60 beats per minute or less.)
- Enya
- Yanni
- Mellow jazz
- Typically, any music without words that cannot be sung (and therefore distracting) will work

Strategies to Assist with Memorization

Paper and Pencil Strategies

- Have students print information to be memorized.

- Border key spelling words, people, places, etc. (See example below.)

- Have students use two colors when working, alternating the color of each fact they are writing in their notes. Color makes facts stand out as unique. If all notes are in one color, nothing stands out as unique and is therefore harder to remember.

- Highlight important information.

- Alternate color of bullets using gel pens, markers, crayons, etc.

Mind & Body Connection Strategies

- Use movement to enhance memory.

- Act out vocabulary words.

- Come up with a gesture to represent key people, places, or things.

- Use sign language.

- If you can take students to the gym, make a game out of spelling a word then shooting a basket. It doesn't matter what rules you make up. What is important is the movement, fun, and challenge in the activity.

- If you like football, soccer, or any other sports better, use that sport as a foundation. Make your own rules. As long as spelling, etc. is part of the game rules, it will be effective.

- Hop & Chunk Spelling – Students spell out a word and jump between each chunk of the word.

Break a word into spelling "chunks" and hop while spelling each chunk. E.g.: Maneuver = Man (hop) eu (hop) ver (hop)

Vocabulary Strategy

- **Choose a Vocabulary Word**
  - Print it
  - Border it
- **Ask your child to tell meaning**
- **Reinforce correct definition**
- **Stand and act out movement for word while spelling word out loud three times!**

Teaching Each Other

- Students are pre-arranged in pairs.
- Assign partner A and partner B.
- Teach 10 minutes — stop.
- Set timer for 1-2 minutes.
- Partner A teach Partner B one thing that you have taught them in the past 10 minutes.
- Set timer for 1-2 minutes.
- Class shares what they learned.
- Repeat for one more round.

Marker Boards: So That All May Participate!

Active participation enhances memory. This strategy engages each student in the review process.

Every student in the group has a

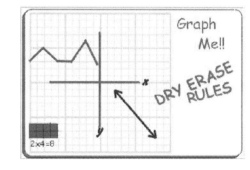

- Whiteboard
- Dry-erase marker or wipe off crayon
- Little kid sock (for wiping and storing marker or crayon)

Paraprofessional asks a question.
Students write answers on whiteboards.
After fair amount of time, students are asked to hold up their boards showing their answers.

- The paraprofessional can see how ALL students in the group are doing in one look.
- It stops blurters.
- Allows those that need processing time to finally get it!

Music as a Strategy

The brain processes and remembers music differently than it processes and remembers spoken words and symbols. Using music to memorize information is a highly effective strategy that is grievously underutilized. Advertisers use music in product jingles to promote their products. They do it because the jingles help us "remember" their product when shopping. Parents can use this strategy with their students to help them memorize key information needed for tests, quizzes, and general knowledge. Students as young as two years old can be taught to remember their name, address, and phone number to music. Singing is a powerful memory tool.

- Link old tunes with new concepts
- Pick a popular song and rewrite the lyrics of the song to match the information to be memorized.
- Rap it! Chant it! Clap it!

Here are some examples:
Quadratic Equation to the Tune of "Pop! Goes the Weasel."
x e-quals neg-a-tive b
plus or minus the squaaaare root
of b squared minus fouuur a c
all over twooo a

Helping Verbs to the Tune of "Mary Had a Little Lamb"
Is, are, was, were, am, be, been
Have, has, had
Do, did, does
May, might, mu-ust,
Can, will, shall,
Could, would, should, being

Mind Mapping/Graphic Roadmaps/Visual Organizers

I started using mind mapping after reading *I Can See You Naked: A Fearless Guide To Making Great Presentations* by Ron Hoff (1988). My first presentation was drawn out like a colorful board game with a route to follow, arrows, and picture images of what I was going to do decorating the path. I remember thinking how much easier it was to use than index cards with a text script written on them. It also was much less restricting. I didn't feel tied to reading the cards. Rather, I looked at the picture and went from memory. It saved me from the plight of many presenters: that of being tied to a script.

The technique worked so well for me that I started expanding the idea into my teaching efforts. **As I read selections from English texts to my students, I drew the events out on paper in map and graphic format.** I would often interject silly ditties and exclamations of passion into the effort to make what I was reading to them stick out in their memory. Given my students were at the 'cool' age of 'teen' they would often look at me and say, "You are crazy!" My pat answer was always, "Yes, I am, but you'll remember this because of it." And they did.

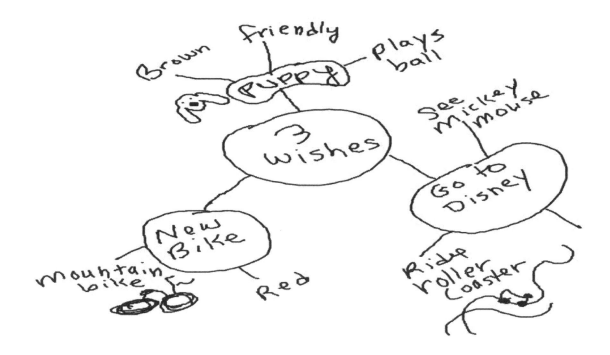

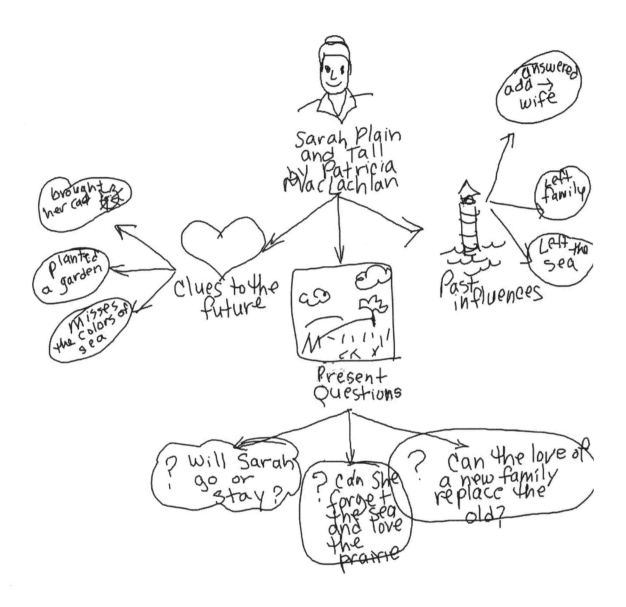

Students learn and remember mind maps better if they create them out of their own mental images and patterns. One can define a mind map as follows: A mind map consists of a central word or concept, around which you draw the 5 to 10 main ideas that relate to that central word. You then take each of those 'new' words and again draw the 5 to 10 main ideas that relate to each of those words.

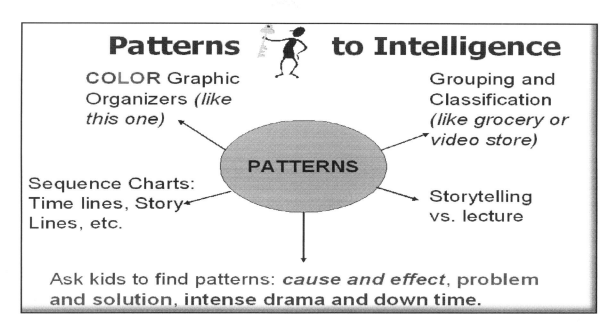

Mnemonic Devices[9]

Mnemonic. n. A device, such as a formula or rhyme, used as an aid in remembering.

Mnemonics, or the science or art of aiding memory, is an ancient concept. Many people rely on mnemonic devices to help remember what they have learned or need to recall, from grocery lists, to people's names, to kings and queens, or the presidents. What works for one person may not work for another. The following five memory devices help to improve retention of information.

Some examples of mnemonics:
- I AM A PERSON: The four Oceans (Indian, Arctic, Atlantic, and Pacific).

- HOMES: Huron, Ontario, Michigan, Erie, and Superior: the Great Lakes in North America.

The best are those made up by the student, as they are meaningful to him/her.

Associations

Developing associations is a familiar strategy used to recall information by connecting it to other, more familiar pieces of information. For example,

---

[9] Adapted from the work of Michael DiSpezio, author of Critical Thinking Puzzles (Sterling, 1996) for Scientific American Frontiers. http://www.pbs.org/saf/4_class/45_pguides/pguide_703/4573_trufalse.html

memorizing a sequence of seemingly random digits is easy when that number series is your birth date or street address. Developing associations is also a helpful way to remember new information.

Rhyming

Rhymes and jingles are powerful memory devices. Just think how often you have used the rhyme, "Thirty days has September..." to recall the number of days within a month.

To use the Rhyme Technique all you have to do is make up a rhyme to remember what you want to remember! It is fun! If you are musically inclined, you can even make up whole songs to help you remember long pieces of important information.

Examples:
30 days has September
April, June, and November

In 1492, Columbus sailed the ocean blue.

In 1903, the Wright brothers flew free.
First successful flight

I before E except after C
And when saying "A" as in Neighbor or Weigh
And weird is weird.

Chunking

When reciting a telephone or Social Security number, most people are apt to speak it in three chunks. For example, the first and second chunks of a phone number consist of three digits and the third chunk contains four digits. Chunking the numbers makes a meaningless series easier to remember. Can you think of other series of numbers that are frequently chunked?

800-566-3712

Mnemonic for this phone number is: Five people watched while big bully 7 blocked 3 from taking his place with friends 1 & 2.

Chunking is also an excellent strategy for remembering how to spell words. An example of chunking follows:

Other examples of chunked spelling words:

ALBU   QUER   QUE
RE   NUMER   ATION
PENN   SYLVAN   IA
CZ   ECHO   SLO   VAKIA
LEU   KE   MIA
FRE   NET   IC
REC EIVE

Acronyms

An acronym is a word formed from the initial letter or letters of each of the parts of a name or organization. For example, the acronym **LASER** stands for **L**ight **A**mplification by **S**timulated **E**mission of **R**adiation. Some other familiar acronyms are **RADAR**, **REM** sleep, **SCUBA**, **SONAR**, **NASA**, **ZIP** code, etc. You can also make up acronyms to help you remember information. Think of an acronym as a "fun" word or phrase in which each letter stands for the first letter of the item to be recalled.

Acrostics

An acrostic is a memory strategy similar to an acronym, but it takes the first letters of a series of words, lines, or verses to form a memorable phrase. Sometimes the phrase is nonsense, which may help you remember it! Here are two: **K**ing **P**hilip **C**ame **O**ver **F**or **G**randma's **S**oup or **K**ings **P**lay **C**ards **O**n **F**at **G**reen **S**tools. Each acrostic stands for the biological classification hierarchy (**K**ingdom, **P**hylum, **C**lass, **O**rder, **F**amily, **G**enus, and **S**pecies).

Example of mnemonics combined with meaningful pictures that use associations:

Taxonomy

King Philip Came Over For Grandma's Soup.
- Kingdom
- Phylum
- Class
- Order
- Family
- Genus
- Species

© AIMHI Ed Programs

Sequencing Strategy

Use adding machine tape to create a visual storyline, timeline or sequence to be memorized:

Drawing, Color, and Memory

Simply put, we remember what we see in color better than what we see in black and white. According to Eric Jensen in *Brain-Based Learning* (1996), we remember colors first and content next. Colors affect us on physiological and psychological levels.

- Add color to homework paperwork.

- Print notes and alternate two colors for each individual point.

- According to the research, color communicates more effectively than black and white. How much more effectively? Here's what the research says:

© 2010 SUSAN FITZELL, M. Ed.

- o Color visuals increase willingness to read by up to 80 percent.[10]
- o Using color can increase motivation and participation by up to 80 percent.[3]
- o Color enhances learning and improves retention by more than 75 percent.[11]
- o Color accounts for 60 percent of the acceptance or rejection of an object and is a critical factor in the success of any visual experience.[12]

The Meaning of Color

Red - An engaging and emotive color, which can stimulate hunger or excite and disturb the individual.
Yellow - The first color distinguished by the brain.
Blue - Calms a tense person and increases feelings of well-being.
Green - A calming color, like blue.
Brown - Promotes a sense of security and relaxation and reduces fatigue.

Draw It So You'll Know It

Have your students draw pictures of what they are reading.
Have youth illustrate their notes with drawings that represent what is in the notes.

This drawing is actually done in color markers. All pictures used in this handbook were originally done in color.

---

[10] The Persuasive Properties of Color; Ronald E. Green; Marketing Communications, October 1984.

[11] Loyola University School of Business, Chicago, IL., as reported in Hewlett-Packard's Advisor, June 1999; (http://www.hpadvisor.com).

[12] The Power of Color; Dr. Morton Walker; Avery Publishing Group; 1991.

Drill and Practice Strategies

The Fitzpell Method of Studying Spelling Words

Option 1: Use phonics rules to determine which letters should be in a **standout color**.

These cards are actually done in color markers. All pictures used in this handbook were originally done in color.

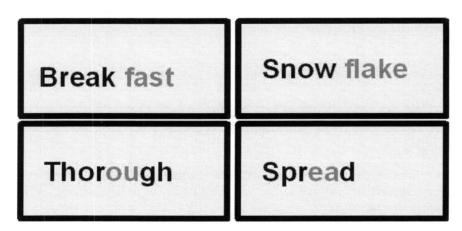

Option 2: Pre-test. Use pre-test errors to determine which letters should be in a **stand-out color**. Make the corrected mistake in spelling stand out so that the mistake is not repeated.

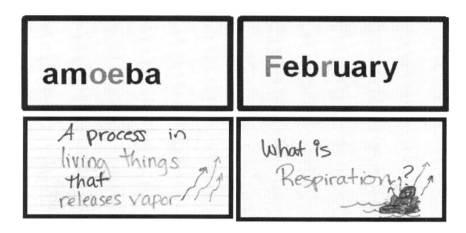

Whenever possible, add clip art pictures to 'visualize' the word.
Use bright color markers with good contrast to differentiate.
Add any other symbols, sound cues, etc. to make the spelling word more memorable.

PRINT the words on INDEX CARDS.
Practice by running through the cards 2-3 times each day for the four days before the spelling test. Put aside the cards that need more study. Cards that can be spelled quickly can be pulled out of the daily second and third run.

Option 3: Put the key words in the question and the key words in the answer in a different color than the rest of the text.

Good luck! You should see a significant improvement in spelling test grades.

Three Card Match: Review

Materials
Index Cards: Choose three of the following card colors: pink, green, blue, yellow, or white. If you only have white cards or white paper, color-code the cards.

For example:
Put a yellow dot or stripe on the word cards.
Put a green dot or stripe on the picture cards.
Put a pink dot or stripe on the definition cards...and so on and so forth.

Pictures
Of the item being reviewed, or related to the concept being reviewed, or mnemonic pictures to form an association

Instructions
1. Break down what they have to memorize into three related concepts, facts, pictures, meanings, etc.
2. Each card should contain one 'item.' (See example below.)

An enormous mammal with a very long nose called a trunk.

3. Label the back of each card in a set with a number so students can turn the card over and self-correct.

For example:
The word elephant, the picture of the elephant and the definition of the elephant would all be numbered #1 on the back.

The word zebra, the picture of the zebra and the definition of the zebra would all be numbered #2, etc.

Options for use:
Students can match the cards on their own as a review in the resource room or classroom. If they have their own sets, they may use them at home to study.

▪ Students can pair up to match the cards. This is an excellent peer tutoring activity.

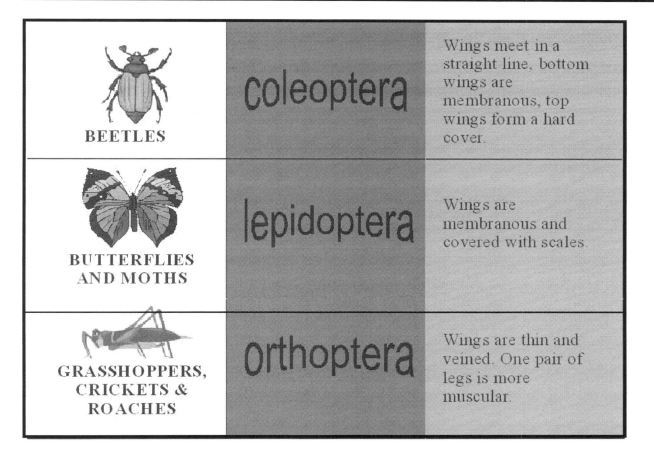

▪ ▪ Visual or Mnemonic ▪	▪ ▪ Word	▪ ▪ Definition
▪	▪ ▪ Folium of Descartes	▪ ▪ x^3 + y^3 = 3x*y

	coleoptera	Wings meet in a straight line, bottom wings are membranous, top wings form a hard cover.
BEETLES		
BUTTERFLIES AND MOTHS	lepidoptera	Wings are membranous and covered with scales.
GRASSHOPPERS, CRICKETS & ROACHES	orthoptera	Wings are thin and veined. One pair of legs is more muscular.

Make it Meaningful

By **Bringing Emotion into the Lesson**

We remember things that evoke our emotion. Advertisers use this knowledge effectively. When we can bring drama into the classroom, we will see increased learning.

- Make it a story.
- Read with dramatization.
- Use a gripping picture to engage discussion.

Whenever possible, introduce concepts with pictures that evoke emotions. Many times, we focus on the printed word in texts and make minimal use of the photos. Artwork and drama reach the heart. Use it whenever possible to hook your students into the lesson.

Note: Use Photos as Tools for Brain-Based Learning and Multiple Intelligences

Strategies to Assist with Writing Assignments

Writing Strategies

Strategy for Getting "Un-stuck" While Writing: **Clustering**

The clustering activity detailed on the following pages helps students who are struggling to write an essay as well as young adults filling out college applications.

Clustering Activity Step One

If the student has to write a paper, instruct him/her to draw a big circle on a piece of paper.

Put the topic of the paper in the center of the circle. Note: If there is more than one topic, you might have more than one circle. For example, writing about three wishes will require three circles — one for each wish.

Instruct the student to write any thoughts, ideas, and feelings about the topic in the circle. Also, ask questions about the topic or draw pictures of ideas.

Do not worry about spelling, grammar, sentences, etc. at this point. The purpose is to get the ideas out. Worry about writing rules later.

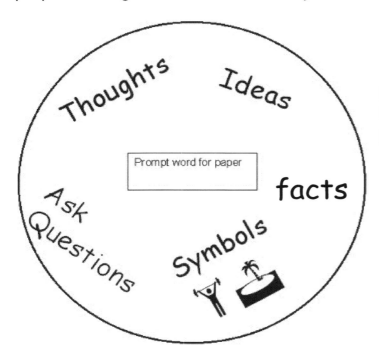

Make this circle BIG — at least the size of an 8" X 8" piece of paper.

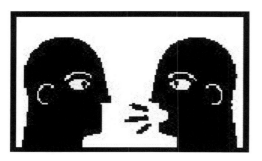

After students "create" in the circle, allow them to share what they have written with a partner.

Clustering Step Two

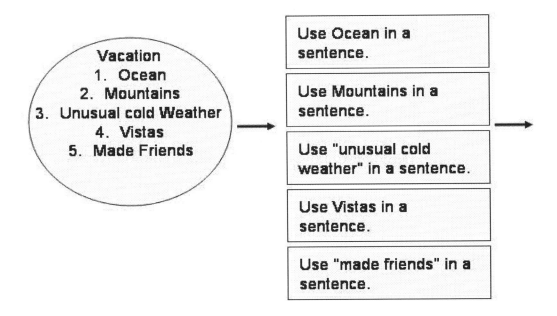

Instruct students to take the "best" words and ideas from inside their circle and use each word in a sentence.
This sentence will be the topic sentence for the paragraphs they will write.
Write the sentences on strips of lined notepaper or lined sticky Post-It® notes.

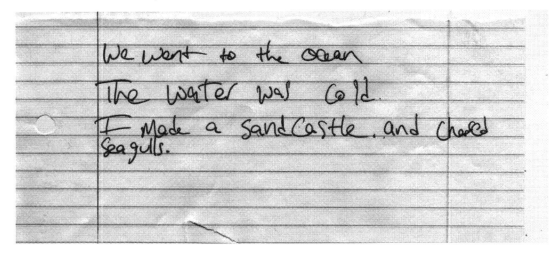

Clustering Step Three

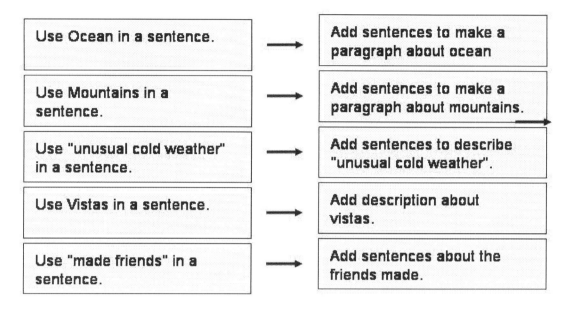

Use Ocean in a sentence.	→ Add sentences to make a paragraph about ocean
Use Mountains in a sentence.	→ Add sentences to make a paragraph about mountains.
Use "unusual cold weather" in a sentence.	→ Add sentences to describe "unusual cold weather".
Use Vistas in a sentence.	→ Add description about vistas.
Use "made friends" in a sentence.	→ Add sentences about the friends made.

Now, take each sentence and add a few more sentences about the topic sentence on that strip of paper.
Try to write two or three more sentences about the topic sentence.

*NOTE: Do not worry about spelling, grammar, or punctuation at this point in the exercise. Worrying about the rules makes it more difficult to be creative.

Clustering Step Four

Add sentences to make a paragraph about ocean	**Add Introduction**
Add sentences to make a paragraph about mountains.	
Add sentences to describe "unusual cold weather".	Add
Add description about vistas.	
Add sentences about the friends made.	**Add Conclusion**

Next, add an introduction and conclusion on separate strips of lined paper.

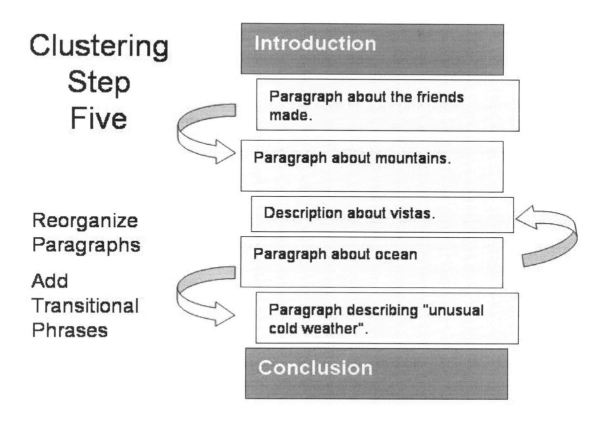

Next, move the strips of paper around so that the paper is in the best order and makes the most sense.

This process allows the writer to start anywhere in the paper. It frees up creative thought and encourages the process to start. Organizing the paper after paragraphs are written is easy.

Scotch® tape all the strips on one or two big pieces of paper.

Add transition words to make the paragraphs flow together.

Examples of **Transition Words**

To Add:
And, again, and then, besides, equally important, finally, further, furthermore, nor, too, next, lastly, what's more, moreover, in addition, first (second, etc.)

To Compare:
Whereas, but, yet, on the other hand, however, nevertheless, on the other hand, on the contrary, by comparison, where, compared to, up against, balanced against, but, although, conversely, meanwhile, after all, in contrast, although this may be true

To Prove:
Because, for, since, for the same reason, obviously, evidently, furthermore, moreover, besides, indeed, in fact, in addition, in any case, that is

To Show Exception:
Yet, still, however, nevertheless, in spite of, despite, of course, once in a while, sometimes

To Show Time:
Immediately, thereafter, soon, after a few hours, finally, then, later, previously, formerly, first (second, etc.), next, and then

To Repeat:
In brief, as I have said, as I have noted, as has been noted

To Emphasize:
Definitely, extremely, obviously, in fact, indeed, in any case, absolutely, positively, naturally, surprisingly, always, forever, perennially, eternally, never, emphatically, unquestionably, without a doubt, certainly, undeniably, without reservation

To Show Sequence:
First (second, etc.), A (B, etc.), next, then, following this, at this time, now, at this point, after, afterward, subsequently, finally, consequently, previously, before this, simultaneously, concurrently, thus, therefore, hence, next, and then, soon

To Give an Example:
For example, for instance, in this case, in another case, on this occasion, in this situation, take the case of, to demonstrate, to illustrate, as an illustration, to illustrate

To Summarize or Conclude:
In brief, on the whole, summing up, to conclude, in conclusion, as I have shown, as I have said, hence, therefore, accordingly, thus, as a result, consequently, on the whole

Clustering Step Six

Rewrite or type into one continuous draft on full sheets of paper.

Hand in draft for teacher to correct.

Introduction
Paragraph about the friends made.
Paragraph about mountains.
Description about vistas.
Paragraph about ocean
Paragraph describing "unusual cold weather".
Conclusion

If the teacher is not correcting a draft, you might help the student with this step.

Clustering Step Seven

Student writes final draft incorporating teacher corrections, feedback and edits.

My Vacation
By Successful Student
Interesting new friends became the focal point of ....
The mountains were...
The vistas were inspiring as mountains met the ocean in a clash of green and aquamarine...
Unfortunately there was an unusual cold weather front....
Overall, the vacation was...

This is the place where the student uses the rules and makes sure that spelling, grammar, and punctuation are correct.

Method for Writing Better Sentences

Write a simple sentence:

_____

_____

Are there any words that can be made more specific? Add words to the chart below that could be used to make your sentence even better.

Who?	What?	When?	Where?	Why?

Now write your new improved sentence

_____

_____

_____

_____

Is there another way this sentence could begin?

_____

_____

_____

Strategies to Assist with Reading Assignments

Highlighting activity

Put Prompts on Materials (or teach students to do it)

- Simple prompts on materials can help students succeed.

 Star at the starting point.

Arrow to indicate direction.

𝕾𝕿𝕬𝕽𝕿 𝕳𝕰𝕽𝕰 ✓ Green mark to keep going

- Bullets

This is a strategy to teach students how to dissect and highlight an assignment so they "remember" all the parts.

When reviewing an assignment with a student, use highlighters and color markers to dissect the information on the assignment.

These prompts are presented in different colors. The simple act of picking up different color highlighters or markers works to keep students involved and attentive.

Post-It® Note Method of "Highlighting"

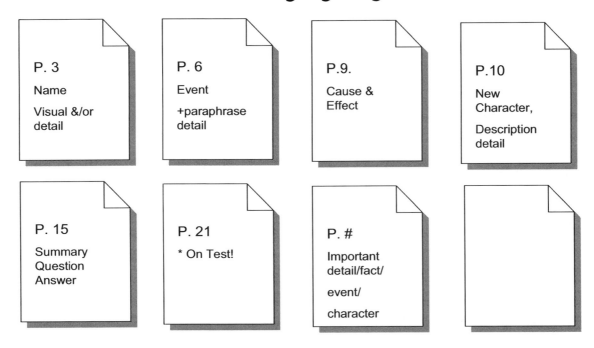

P. 3

Name

Visual &/or detail

P. 6

Event

+paraphrase detail

P.9.

Cause & Effect

P.10

New Character,

Description detail

P. 15

Summary Question Answer

P. 21

* On Test!

P. #

Important detail/fact/

event/

character

As students are reading a text, every time an important fact, item, cause and effect situation, etc., comes up, have students put a post-it note right in that spot and write the page number, the item and a visual or some detail.

☐

After the chapter is read, the novel is finished, the text section is done, students should take all the Post-it notes and line them up sequentially (as in the picture above) on a sheet of 8½" X 11" paper.

• Place the paper in a sleeve protector.
• Students now have a study guide that is tied to the text.

Math Tip for Spatial Difficulties

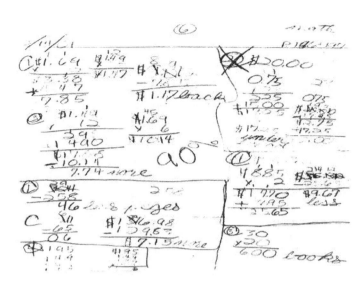

Are you tired of seeing math problems all jumbled up on an unlined piece of paper? Does it cause your student to make mistakes because numbers and equations are not lined up properly? Here's a simple solution!

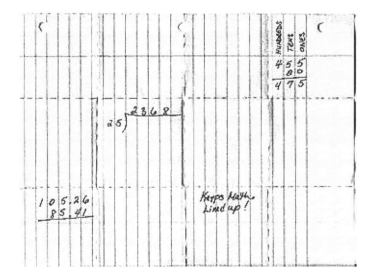

- Keep math lined up!
- Turn standard lined paper sideways.
- Grid paper also works very well. Make your own grid paper with enlarged grids.

Making Assignments Easier to Accomplish

The forms on the following pages give students the structure, lines, and space to be successful with current event assignments, book reports, etc.

They are not only ready-made adaptations that you may photocopy and use with your students; they are examples of handouts that are designed for student success.

What makes these handouts work?

☐ Font size is 14pt +

☐ San serif font

☐ Good use of white space

☐ Lines for students to write their answers

☐ Prompts to trigger recall of required information

☐ Structure and organization

☐ Clearly defined expectations

When adapting handouts for students, used these forms as models of how handouts should be designed for success.

Current Events

Circle one: World   Nation   Local

<u>Do this</u>: Find an article from a newspaper that is interesting to you. Answer the following questions about the article. Attach the article or a photocopy.

Cite your source: _____

Who is the story about? (Your answer could be a group of people, an organization, or one person.)

_____

About what event or happening does the article tell?

_____

_____

_____

_____

Where did this event happen? (A city, a state, a building, or an area)

_____

When did the event reported on in the article take place? (Time, a specific day or date, or a reference to a time — yesterday, last week, etc.)

_____

Why did the event in the article happen? (Does your story explain what may have caused this to happen?)

_____

_____

What is your opinion about this article?

_____

_____

_____

Book Report

Title of Book: _____

Author: _____

Illustrator: _____

Publishing Co. & Place of Publication: _____

Copyright Date: _____

Type of Story: Mystery, historical fiction, science fiction, adventure, biography

_____

TIME
Historical period: (Medieval age, Victorian age, Early America, 1900s, etc.)

_____

Duration: (Over what period of time does the story take place? One day, several weeks, 100 years, etc.)

_____

PLACE
Geographical location:

_____

Scenes: (Where does most of the story take place? Examples: outdoors, in someone's home, in a magician's castle)

_____

MAIN CHARACTER
Name:

_____

Physical description: (What does he/she look like?)

_____

_____

Personality description: (What makes him/her special?)

_____

_____

_____

How does this character change during the story?

_____

_____

What feelings does he/she go through?

_____

_____

_____

THE CONFLICTS IN THE STORY (The conflicts are the problems or hard decisions that the characters had to make.)

CONFLICTS/PROBLEMS	HOW DID YOUR CHARACTER DEAL WITH THE PROBLEMS?
1	
2	
3	

TELL SOME OF THE EXCITING THINGS THAT YOUR CHARACTER DID AND HOW HIS OR HER PERSONALITY MADE THESE PARTS EXCITING.

_____

_____

_____

_____

_____

YOUR OPINION OF THIS STORY:

What did you like about it?

_____

_____

What didn't you like about it?

_____

_____

PROJECT PLANNING CHART

NAME: _____

💡 **Project Topic**

🕐 **Date Due**

I will present the project by doing...

_____ **will proof read my project**
(Hint: pick someone who can spell)

I will need the following materials

_____

_____

_____

I will look for information in the following places

_____

_____

_____

_____

_____

Copyright 2000 by Susan Fitzell   Created with Inspiration Software

Study Tools and Organizers

Note-Taking Strategies

Cut and Paste Notes Using Mind Maps and Charts

- ☐ Consider the graphic organizer on the following page and the different ways it can be used to differentiate:

- ☐ Whenever you are presenting a "process," show the process visually in a process map. This will help the students to visually see what you are teaching and will enhance memory of the process.

- ☐ Give students a process map or a graphic organizer with blank boxes.

- ☐ Have students fill in the key words as you teach about the topic.

- ☐ Give students a grid of the key words, a glue stick, and scissors. Have them cut out the words.

- ☐ Then as you re-teach the lesson, instruct students to move the words to the correct box and paste them down.

- ☐ Then as you review the lesson, instruct students to move the words to the correct box and paste them down.

- ☐ Power of Two: Instruct students to work together to decide where the words go on the map and move the words to the correct box. You might review students' answers and, when correct, instruct them to paste them down.

- ☐ The graphic organizer can be used as a quiz or test, thereby minimizing the difficulty for students who read below grade level. Students show what they know without being hindered by their reading disability.

- ☐ _____

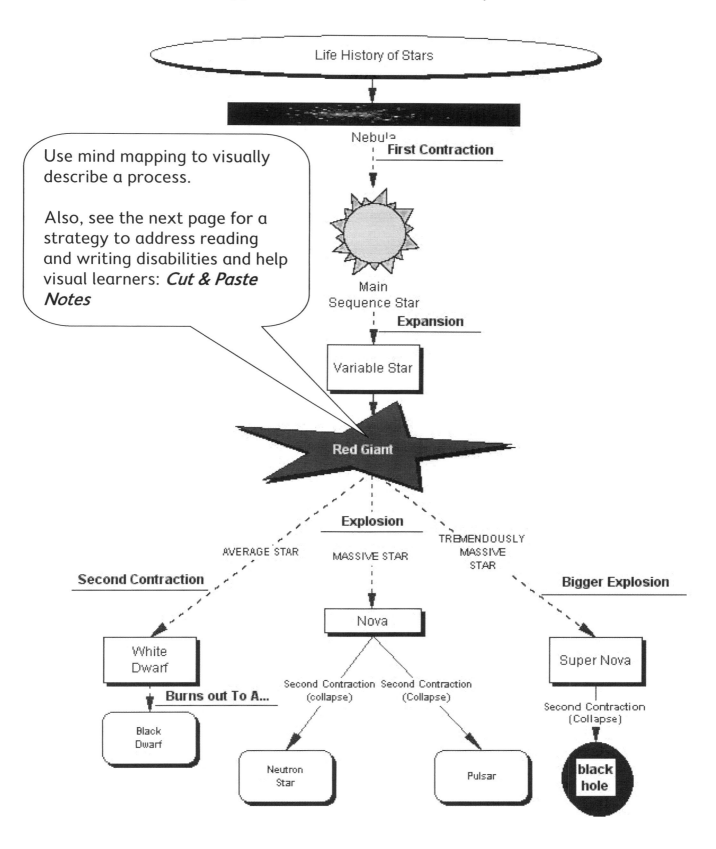

Three-Column Note Paper

BIG IDEAS	DETAILS	TEST QUESTIONS

Team Name: Quarter:

Grade Review Sheet

Name: Class:

ASSIGNMENT	HW	CW	QUIZZES	TESTS
TITLE, DATE, GRADE	%	%	%	%

Include TITLE, DATE, AND GRADE for each assignment received.
This grade list should be kept in the front of your binder!
Graph your grades so you can SEE how you are doing! Use a bar or line graph.

Add Checkboxes:

Hand draw checkboxes on assignments to help a student remember all the steps. Have him or her check them off after they are complete.

Example below:

NAME_____PER_____DATE_____

CONSTELLATION PROJECT CHECKLIST

CHECK OFF EACH ITEM AS YOU COMPLETE IT!

☐ Look up the constellation in a book. (There are books in the library and the science class.)

☐ Draw the pattern of the stars that make it up.

Use plain white paper. Use BLACK ink or pencil. Make it no LARGER than 3½" (height) X 8" (length).

☐ Connect the star patterns with DASHED lines.

☐ Cut out your constellations and mount it on BLACK construction paper at the TOP of the sheet.

☐ Pierce PIN HOLES (not massive holes) through the stars.

☐ Look up the myth about your constellation.

☐ Write the story (myth) in YOUR OWN WORDS.

☐ The final draft should be in PEN on plain WHITE PAPER.

☐ State where the myth comes from.

☐ Mount the myth BELOW your constellation on the black construction paper
(8½" X 11").

Use MSWord Readability Statistics to Improve Writing

If students know what the readability level of their writing is, they can challenge themselves to bring it up higher! Simply use words with more syllables and write longer, more complex sentences. Then spell check again and see if your reading level is higher!

To display readability statistics in MSWord (These instructions are for MSWord 2000):

On the Tools menu, click 'Options', and then click the 'Spelling & Grammar' tab.

Select the 'Check grammar with spelling' checkbox.

Select the 'Show readability statistics' checkbox, then click 'OK'.

Click 'Spelling and Grammar' on the Standard toolbar.

When Word finishes checking spelling and grammar, it displays information about the reading level of the document.

Acknowledgment
Dr. Mary S. Neumann, DHAP, NCHSTP, "Developing Effective Educational Print Materials"

NOTE: In MSWord 2007 Spelling and Grammar tools are customized under the Word Options tool in the main drop down menu.

1. Click on the MS ball in the upper left corner.

2. Click on 'Word Options' at the bottom of the dropdown box.

3. Click on 'Proofing'.

4. At the bottom of the menu box, click on 'Show readability statistics'.

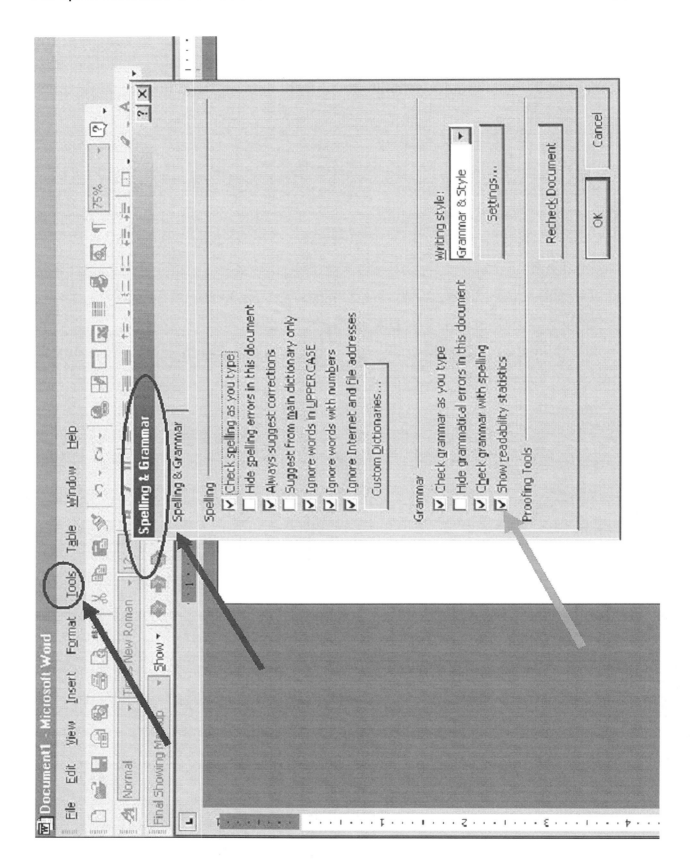

AutoSummarize in MSWord

Use AutoSummarize to highlight key points, create an abstract or a summary of a student's writing. Use it to summarize information that is too long for some students to read. **Note: In MSWord 2007**, you must add 'Autosummary Tools' to your customized shortcut ribbon. Click on 'Help' and search for "Autosummary". Choose "Automatically Summarizes a Document" for instructions.

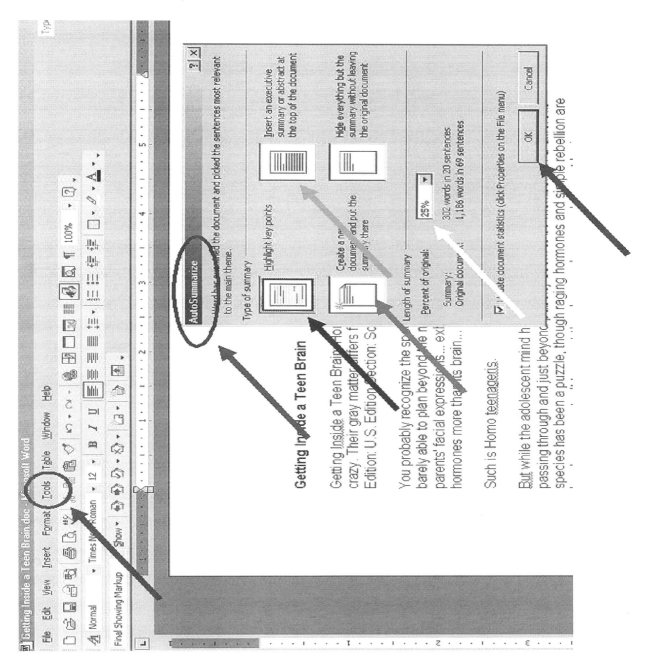

Difficulty/Adaptation Quick List

Difficulty	Adaptation
Poor literacy skills	Provide simpler text/use peer support.
Speech/language difficulty	Check understanding of key words. Partner/group oral work.
Listening/following instructions	Highlight/cue in to important information/provide lists.
Poor numeric skills	Provide apparatus, e.g., counters, algebra manipulatives.
Written work: copying notes, taking notes from lecture, etc.	Use alternative forms of recording.
Grasping/retaining new concepts	Give more practice. Use smaller steps. Use alternative language. Use memory strategies.
Difficulty with maps/graphs/charts	Tracing photocopy. Copy and enlarge, add color/shading.
Short concentration span/keeping on task	Provide short tasks, frequent verbal cues.
Distracts others/is distracted	Sit in front, isolate from others, explore supportive groups.
Working independently	Pair with responsible partner.
Keeping classroom code of conduct	Give positive reinforcement. Diary of specific incidents.
Relating to other pupils	Change seating position or group. Monitor triggers.
Working in cooperation with others	Pair with responsible partner. Define group rules.
Relating positively to adults	Be a role model. Negotiate one-to-one.
Slow-paced work	Realistic deadlines. Allow extra time.
Handwriting/presentation difficulties	Allow extra time and/or alternative ways of recording.
Low self-esteem/lack of confidence	Notice positives. Plan for success/achievement, give classroom responsibilities.
Organizational skills	Encourage use of lists, routines, labels, study buddies.
Homework	Time to explain homework in lesson. Time for class to record assignment. Use parental support.
Becoming upset at difficulties	Notice positives. Reassure.

World Wide Web Resources

American Federation of Teachers Paraprofessional and School-Related Personnel Web site www.aft.org/psrp/

Minnesota Paraprofessional Consortium
University of Minnesota
111 Pattee Hall; 150 Pillsbury Drive SE
Minneapolis, MN 55455
612-624-9893
Web site: http://ici2.umn.edu/para/

Montana Paraeducator Development Project
Montana State University at Billings
Web site: http://www.msubillings.edu/cspd/pararesources.htm

National Resource Center for Paraprofessionals in Education and Related Services
Utah State University
Logan, UT 84322-6526
435-797-7272
Web site: http://www.nrcpara.org

The PAR²A Center
University of Colorado at Denver
Contact: Dr. Nancy French, Director
Web site: http://www.paracenter.org/PARACenter/
The Center provides the Paraeducator Supervision Academy, comprehensive curriculum packages for paraeducators serving English Language Learners, students with low-incidence disabilities, and many more professional development opportunities.

Paraeducator.com
Web site: http://www.paraeducator.com/
A resource for paraeducators in Washington state. Includes training modules in the core competencies for paraeducators, online discussion groups, and fact sheets concerning new Title I requirements.

Order Susan's Books!

Cogent Catalyst Publications
an AIMHI Educational Programs partner company

Customer information
Name:
Street:
City, State & Zip:
Phone 1:
Phone 2:
Email Address:

Order Date:

Mail orders to PO Box 6182, Manchester, NH 03018 or Fax to (603) 218-6291 * Contact us at info@cogentcatalyst.com * 603-625-6087

Shipping & Handling

Order Total	Shipping Price
Up to $55.00 (except P	Free Shipping
Large posters (< 10)	$7.95
$55.01 - $70.00	$9.95
$70.01 - $100.00	$11.95
$100.01 - 149.00	$13.95
More than $149.01	10% of Subtotal

All orders are shipped via USPS and can be expected within 14 days of the time we receive your order. Items ordered at one time are shipped together whenever possible.

Qty.	Description	Unit Price	Discounted/Bulk Price	Line Total
	Co-Teaching and Collaboration in the General Classroom 2nd Ed.	$24.97		
	Set of 10: Co-Teaching and Collaboration		$199.97	
	Free the Children: Conflict Education for Strong, Peaceful Minds	$15.95		
	Set of 10: Free the Children		$124.97	
	Paraprofessionals and Teachers Working Together 2nd Edition	$24.97		
	Set of 10: Paraprofessionals and Teachers		$199.97	
	Please Help Me With My Homework: English 2nd Edition	$10.97		
	Set of 10: Please Help Me		$87.97	
	Please Help Me With My Homework: Spanish	$10.97		
	Set of 10: Please Help Me		$87.97	
	Special Needs in the General Classroom 2nd Edition	$24.97		
	Set of 10: Special Needs		$199.97	
	Transforming Anger to Personal Power	$23.95		
	Set of 10: Transforming Anger		$199.97	
	Umm Studying? What's That?	$15.00		
	Set of 10: Umm Studying?		$119.97	
	Memorization & Test Taking Strategies DVD Training Program	$895.00		
	Flash Cards: Special Needs in the General Classroom	$7.95		
	Flash Cards: Umm Studying... What's That?	$7.95		
	Poster- MOODZ: Laminated 8 1/2" x 11"	$4.95		
	Poster-MOODZ: Gloss Coverstock 18" x 24"	$9.95		
	Poster-Feed The Future One Drop at a Time 15" X 11" (standard size)	$9.95		
	Poster Set-Response to Intervention	$29.95		
	Resource CD: Ready-Made Forms & Tools 2010	$9.95		
	Sticky Notes "Best Ideas"	$2.50		
	Write-In:			
	Write-In:			
	Write-In:			
			Subtotal:	
			Shipping & Handling:	
			Total:	

****Large posters require shipping because of tube mailers

The portion below must be filled out or your order will not be processed

☐Cash   ☐Check   ☐Visa/MC
Visa/MC#_____   Exp.Date: _____

Make checks payable to Susan Fitzell

Notes

28407811R00087

Made in the USA
Charleston, SC
12 April 2014